Queen of the Ritz

Queen of The Ritz

Samuel Marx

The Bobbs-Merrill Company, Inc.
INDIANAPOLIS/NEW YORK

Copyright © 1978 by Samuel Marx

All rights reserved, including the right of reproduction in whole or in part in any form
Published by The Bobbs-Merrill Company, Inc.
Indianapolis   New York

Designed by Rita Muncie
Manufactured in the United States of America

First printing

Library of Congress Cataloging in Publication Data

Marx, Samuel, 1902–
   Queen of the Ritz.

   1. Auzello, Blanche.   2. Auzello, Claude.
3. Hotel management—France—Paris—Biography.
4. Ritz Hotel, Paris.   I. Title.
TX910.5.A95M37   647'.944'360922 ‹B›   78-55639
ISBN 0-672-52316-7

To Blanche and Claude . . .
who remembered it like this

Acknowledgments

A large bouquet of thanks is due many whose observations supported the memories of Blanche and Claude.

In Nice and Monte Carlo, members of the Auzello family —Francette Combe, Jean Graniou, and Jean Giaume —filled in details that Claude was too modest to relate. Elise and Yvonne Mazaye, who now live in Chatel-Guyon, contributed essential memorabilia. The same is true of Kitty Hemsley, Mary Rosenthal, Selma Jenny, and my good friend Thomas Quinn Curtiss in Paris.

In London, Lady Anne Hughes, David Lewin, and Stephen Watt. In the United States, Anita Loos, Kitty (Mrs. Omar N.) Bradley, Foxy Sondheim, Ina Vestal, Beth Wendel, Doris Kenyon Mlynarski, Rubye de Remer, Irene Hayman, Ruth Dubonnet, and J. Ainsworth Morgan, as well as Justus Lawrence, Dr. Hank Ross, and Jimmy Green, who were with the United States Army when Paris was liberated.

From Blanche's family, her nieces Nancy Frankel, Doris Frankel, and Carolyn Robbins assisted with loving recall, as did Herman Ruby's widow Betty. Also my sons Kenneth and Richard—they knew Blanche only in her later years and found her absolutely baffling. She introduced them as her nephews on the theory that ties to small boys made her appear younger.

I regret that Charley Ritz, who contributed many vivid reminiscences, did not live until publication. Marie Louise Ritz verified the quotes Claude attributed to her. Among others who personally saw to the splendor of the Ritz during the Auzello years, I am grateful to Bernard Penché, Januscz Zymbruskie, and Georges Scheuer. The manuscript was almost complete when the hotel passed to Monique Ritz, widow of Charley, who brought me together with Mouton and Laberenne, staff members during the war and still there in 1978. Charley Ritz knew there would be disclosures that he hoped would remain untold, but neither he nor anyone else restricted the writing.

Lastly, I am indebted to June Levant, Lynne Spaulding, and Gene Rachlis for much-needed editorial suggestions, and their names belong close to mine.

Samuel Marx
Cheviot Hills, California

Foreword

In the course of her life—and she was past seventy when her husband shot and killed her—Blanche changed her hair to every known color except one—grey.

She was brunette originally, and occasionally after, but it was the color of gold more than others. She kept it long and flowing, so she could whip it into the air and around her face when she shook her head. She shook it often. All the boys noticed it and remembered. She knew that, of course. They also thought her as sassy, stylish and sexy as any girl in the neighborhood. She knew that, too.

She was my mother's youngest sister—there were five; and long before I was taken with the enchantment of women, I was sure my Aunt Blanche must be one of the most gorgeous creatures I would ever see.

Long thin legs could be subtly observed through provocative slit-skirts, topped by a gently rounded figure. Over all, a heart-shaped face with enormous hazel eyes that sparkled with the upturn of her lips. She must have been about seventeen when I first noticed.

She had an elusive smile, impudent and intriguing, one that jolts a man to his roots. It was as if she were privileged to share a private and amusing secret with God, a smile that transcended ordinary beauty, if one may describe beauty as ordinary.

Her smile didn't stay on her lips; it rose to her eyes. A girl who smiles like that fascinates a man, spurring his desires. She remains always in his memory. Any man can conjure in his mind's eye a glimpse of a girl with that smile; it carries with it a wish for a new love, and that in itself is unforgettable. She is a special breed. Her confidence is boundless; she knows her place is assured. The future holds no fears; she is at ease with the world. I didn't know these things about Blanche then; I came to realize them later, for when she was seventeen I was only ten.

Blanche was a precocious tomboy. She wouldn't play with dolls, ignoring her own and those she inherited when her sisters outgrew them. She refused to learn to sew or knit. Dancing a thin line between arrogance and aristocracy, she rejected all lessons intended to enhance her appeal to boys seeking domesticity.

Other girls remained inside the strict borders of convention; she went over the fence. She carried her own pack of "Sweet Caporals" cigarettes, a daring exercise in female emancipation. "She even smokes outdoors!" exclaimed a shocked young suitor. It was commonly believed that a girl who smoked in public would do anything.

Her parents were upset because she joked about marriage instead of embracing it. That puzzled me because I thought her great fun to be with. A single girl, I was told, wasn't supposed to be fun. She had another strike against her: she wanted to work, have a job, a career. A nice girl from a good family couldn't do that and expect to stay nice.

It was only natural for my Aunt Blanche and me to see less of each other as the years moved on and we pursued our personal interests.

Through family channels I heard she was involved with an Egyptian prince, which was exciting and, I thought, added to her fascination. Her sisters, being prim, conventional wives, didn't share my views. I rather suspect they were relieved when she suddenly sailed off to rendezvous with her prince in Paris. If she wouldn't conform, it was better that she go far enough away that the family couldn't see her misbehave.

Our own relationship continued through hit-and-run correspondence, and there was a shift in family pride when her new husband became part of the executive staff of the famous Paris Ritz, although no one knew who he was or how she came to marry him. One didn't engage in a feverish exchange of mail in the 1920s; after all, it took the same time for a letter to get to Paris from America as it does now to get one to the moon.

We've all read or heard about someone called a born musician, a born accountant or a born writer. I have serious doubts if there are such. Someone comes out of the maternity room and says, "It's a boy!" or "It's a girl!" I never heard of a nurse or obstetrician announcing, "It's a writer!"

It was twenty years after I was born before I knew I wanted to write. Then, I decided journalism was my thing.

I was a reporter in autumn, 1927, when Blanche made a triumphal visit to New York, four years after she'd left. She was hardly here a few days before she contended that we Americans were sexually confined and suffering from moral claustrophobia. I understood what she meant.

Only a few weeks before she arrived, Charles Lindbergh touched down at Le Bourget. His nonstop flight from New York to Paris was such an event that the day he came home was pandemonium time. A friendly editor offered me a press badge if I would go down to the harbor area and prowl for anecdotes.

Somewhere along that trail I picked up a story that seemed to be just what he wanted. It had to do with Lindbergh's dislike for his mother. The old lady came unwillingly from her home in Minnesota after a plea from President Coolidge. She didn't care for her son any more than he cared for her. But mother love had to be part of the scene; it was the great American ideal, a tradition set in our earth and water as firmly as the Statue of Liberty.

However, neither of them would agree to a public display of affection. Instead, they sat for ten minutes behind closed doors in the captain's quarters of the cruiser *Memphis* sent to France to fetch him. They sat all alone, rigid, without a word passing between them, not even looking at each other.

It was certainly the sidelight of the day, but it wasn't a scoop, as most of the fellows covering the story heard it, too.

By unanimous agreement, the press killed it. Instead, newspapers and radio reported that with respect to the wishes of mother and son, a loving reunion took place in absolute privacy. Fittingly, it was stated, their tender embraces were shielded from public and photographers. Then the hero emerged to receive the city's acclaim, its reception at City Hall, and 1800 tons of tickertape that showered down on him.

Suppression of the truth disillusioned me with journalism, which I had admired as a bastion of courage. Here were the tops in the country's newsgathering forces knowingly hoodwinking their readers. The day Lindbergh came home changed my life, because, with that revelation clear to me, I looked around for a different form of writing.

Like every reporter of my acquaintance, I thought I could write a better book than anybody, and in searching for characters and a plot, I decided on Blanche and her Egyptian prince. All I needed, I thought, would be a little help from her and a lot from my imagination. So I broached it to her.

She smiled indulgently. I'm sure she must have thought her "kid nephew" would never be able to cut it, but she had time to spend with me, as she wasn't chasing around New York as much as she had expected. Friends she had planned to see had disappeared. Her sisters were busy with their husbands and children. The girls (and men) she could locate disappointed her; their minds had turned provincial, while she had acquired worldliness. After Paris she was finding New York fading into the mists of an uncherished past.

We talked it over at Schrafft's on Fifth Avenue, sitting for two hours over marvelously gooey chocolate sodas.

"Over there, we can do anything we like," she said. "Here, you can't buy a drink—anyway, not in a hotel. You think you have liberty, but you don't."

I admitted ignorance of French freedom but expressed some doubt about it. She was strong in its defense.

"In France your liberty extends as far as the liberty of your neighbor."

That reasoning, she pointed out, allowed more sex in their movies than in ours, nude girls in nightclubs. ("My God, a naked girl is the most beautiful thing in the world! Uhhhh, well, most of them! You've seen some, I suppose?") She was actually annoyed by the modesty of American women. ("Puritans, pure and simple. And I mean *pure!* And I mean *simple, too!*")

American men, too. They lacked boldness and *savoir faire.* It came out then that most French husbands kept mistresses on the side.

Her husband, too? Well, she wasn't disposed to talk about that.

I told her I wanted to fashion a book on her life. I would change the names and write it as fiction, but I wanted the details of her life with the Egyptian prince.

"Listen, you brat, why do you keep on about him? Sure, he was my lover. Maybe if I'd gone to Egypt . . . but I didn't. So write a true story about Popsy and me. And my life at the Ritz."

"Who's Popsy?"

"My husband. He fell for me the minute he saw me. He told people, 'The minute I saw her my heart went pop!'"

I made a note about Popsy. It was the first in a collection of notebooks, letters, fragments of scrap paper—enough to fill a suitcase. But I never got around to that novel. She left New York to live the rest of her life in France, while Hollywood intervened in mine, extending the distance between us another three thousand miles. There were other interventions: the Depression, the gloomy threat of war in Europe, the war itself. The research on the novel I never wrote began forty years before I sat down to do the book she suggested that first day.

Samuel Marx
Cheviot Hills, California

Queen of the Ritz

1

"Luxury stains everyone it touches."
—Charley Ritz

It was the time and the place to be rich, to have social status, to own diamonds and furs and velvet gowns and show them off at the round of balls frequented by the people who counted. The envious poor lined up along the red carpets and watched with awe as the fine-born rich-rich passed through the splendid portals of Fifth Avenue's homes and hotels. Cholly Knickerbocker, the chubby, pompous columnist of Hearst's *New York American* kept his readers well informed on the doings of the Vanderbilts, Astors, Biddles, Goelets, Wideners and Mellons. Less familiar names might creep into those accounts of social events, but the name of Blanche Rubenstein of Manhattan's 110th Street set wasn't among them: you could depend on that.

That time was 1916, when the United States was not yet embroiled in World War I. Blanche was the youngest in the family of seven children born to Sara and Isaac Rubenstein, German-Jewish émigrés who came to New York when they were newlyweds.

Her father was a dapper oddity in the neighborhood. A dark grey Fedora stood straight over his pompadour, a small black mustache jutted from his upper lip, and smoke from a Havana cigar constantly curled from his mouth. A real cute little fellow, he carried a stick for walking instead of for the usual reason—to keep stray dogs away. Blanche loved him dearly and even obeyed him at times.

Her mother adhered to an old-world custom that the five girls should wed in the order of their age. The parade to the altar by her sisters was orderly and methodical. Known throughout the neighborhood for their prettiness, virtue and

1

culinary talents, they made converts out of gentiles. Only Blanche adamantly resisted all efforts to drag her to a stove.

Each favored young man had to pass mother Sara's inspection, presenting his record of past deeds, an inventory of current assets, future prospects, and views on the realities of wedded bliss and the fictions of marital infidelity. There was some heartbreak when a hopeful failed to pass, but Sara waited that out, and the system worked for all but Blanche.

She remained fancy-free and so far as is known took none of the early samplings of sexual gratification that various young men held out to her. She had two brothers who grew up indifferent to matrimony, too.

Her older brother Sylvester was a humorless fellow with a long face and black, bushy eyebrows. He was called Solly because he resented the natural abbreviation to "Sylly." A health nut, he somehow stayed sunburned all year 'round: no mean feat on the sidewalks of New York. A loner and a loser, he would remain a bachelor throughout his gloomy life. As a film salesman he made one notable contribution to Blanche's progress: after weeks of browbeating, he took her to see the studio in New Jersey where the movies he sold were made.

That first look was all she needed. She was sure she could be a film star. "I thought that all I had to have was a brother in the business. They were doing scenes in tiny fragments. You didn't need to act to do those."

When she reported these observations to Solly, he just shrugged sleepily.

Studio acquaintances addressed him as Mr. Ruby. This surprised her. "Only a fool would use his real name in this business," he said, half-philosophically and half-inaccurately. Solly was perennially tired, and taking her to Fort Lee for a day was as far as he would go to thrust her toward a film career. Her lively spirit disturbed him. He and Blanche went on from there without each other, strangers. "A drab existence constitutes Solly's idea of great entertainment," she said.

It was very different with her younger brother. Herman was a joyful extrovert, with ambitions to be a songwriter. He knew little about music but had a gift for rhyming. He haunted Tin

Pan Alley, a phantom region of midtown Manhattan, portrayed so realistically in songs and stories of those days that out-of-towners constantly complained that they couldn't find it on corner lampposts.

He joined a music publishing outfit formed by three songwriters—Waterson, Berlin and Snyder—as a song-plugger, a lowly insect in a busy hive. It was his job to sell his firm's tunes to the minstrels of vaudeville, cabaret and burlesque, demonstrating how the words and music would enhance their acts.

A plugger's greatest asset was a loud voice plus the ability to be emotionally stirred by sad passages or elated with funny lyrics. Herman possessed this. But if he sang on key, it was probably by mistake. Fortunately, his audience usually possessed a similar musical background and wouldn't notice his slip.

Nights, Herman invaded movie theaters ranging from Hoboken to Sheepshead Bay, singing with slides on the screen, urging audiences to join him in the second chorus. Often, Blanche went along to enjoy the show.

It was on one of these nights that Blanche learned that he too had discarded Rubenstein for Ruby.

He laughed off her surprise. "That's no problem for you," he said. "You'll marry a guy who'll change your name. You'll be a Murphy, maybe, or better yet, an Astor or a Vanderbilt."

"Can't you be Rubenstein?"

"In my business, it makes problems."

"It didn't make any for Anton."

"What hits did he write?" That was his chopper, the great conversational riposte of the day. On Tin Pan Alley it could be (and was) hurled sarcastically at the mention of any name from Julius Caesar to Teddy Roosevelt.

"Listen, sis, Irving Berlin changed his name. If it's okay with him, it's okay with me."

It was a significant conversation, because a few years later she eliminated all evidence of being a Rubenstein for reasons she thought okay, too.

Herman enthusiastically plugged his firm's songs to an endless parade of singing waiters and headliners, his lung volume turned high to drown out songs coming through the wall from the publisher next door.

Then, hoarse and exhausted, he would lunch with other pluggers and songwriters. All pluggers wanted to write songs. Lindy's, on the east side of Broadway at 50th Street, was their overcrowded hangout. Its booths held songwriters who had achieved their hopes and those who were still hoping.

One day he invited Blanche to meet the boys, and, as on her visit to the movie studio, she found the atmosphere a heady one. Conversation was fast, jokes were lively, the delicatessen jumped with assorted characters trying to hold the spotlight of one another's attention. Many of the young men Blanche met at Lindy's crowded her for dates. They were lighthearted companions. Sara gave permission to go out with them on condition that Herman chaperone her.

But it was a short-lived period for dating. The United States joined the war against the Kaiser, and the platoon of songwriters marched to a new beat. Herman was among them.

He was inducted at the camp on Long Island where Berlin wrote his revue "Yip, Yip Yaphank!" and was shipped to the front. Herman helped fight World War I from France. Blanche would help fight World War II from the same ravaged land, against the same enemy, twenty-five years later.

In 1917 she stood on Fifth Avenue and sold Liberty Bonds to passersby. She also put in several hours a week at military hospitals, surprisingly stoic when confronted by broken or bloodied bodies.

Germany surrendered in 1918, and Herman came back from France. He worked on a song to be sung with a film starring Mr. and Mrs. Martin Johnson, intrepid hunters whose African adventures had catapulted them to fame.

Theme songs were big then; every new feature had one. During the process of creating it, he often jumped up and locked himself in his room. Finally, it was finished.

"It's a love song," he said. "Safari, I'm coming back to you."

She teased him. Did he think Safari was a girl's name? His face purpled and he rushed back to his room, slamming the door. After a few minutes she asked to see him. He reappeared, calm and agreeable.

"I did war work at Mount Sinai Hospital. Remember?"

Yes. He remembered.

"You're taking dope, aren't you?"

"Don't worry about it, sis. I know what I'm doing. You should see what goes on in the music business. All the guys sniff or smoke or shoot stuff."

"Army doctors will help cure you of the habit."

"Come on, are you kidding? Army doctors? My regiment was full of hopheads. Not me. I take a little snifter now and then. I can handle it."

Blanche had reached the advanced age of twenty-one, and the returned songwriters rushed her more than ever for dates. They gave her a fast glimpse of New York's social life, but glimpses were all they gave her. On their way to Lindy's they passed by celebrated cabaret restaurants—Rector's, Reisenweber's and Churchill's—as beautifully gowned women entered with immaculately groomed escorts. Blanche couldn't help but notice, and notice she did. High society was obviously a magnificent circle in which to whirl. Its comings and goings, swank affairs, debuts, marriages, divorces, games, tournaments and travels occupied many pages of the New York papers.

But the nearest she came to a swank Fifth Avenue affair was a replica on a movie set, for she was trying to make a living as a film actress, using the professional name Blanche Ross. "I'm a good actress," she said. "And I'm going to be a great one."

Film studios in the East were mainly at Fort Lee, New Jersey, a ferry trip across the Hudson and a trolley ride to the top of the Palisades. They made silent movies in those days, of course, cranked out in glass-covered stages.

She loved the excitement on the set and was willing to work as an extra to provide atmosphere, another figure in a crowd. It was, at times, a boring job, with nothing to do but wait while the director focused closeups of the principals. But being discovered in a crowd was often how one got to be a principal.

While working in the popular serial *The Perils of Pauline,* Blanche was introduced to its star, Pearl White, a thin, wistful girl with big eyes and a little acting talent. Their chemistry blended, and what began as idle conversation on a movie set grew into a firm friendship. It developed during and immediately after the war, when Pearl reached the peak of her success.

Her daredevil antics on the screen gave her special appeal. More often than not, she was tied to a railroad track in front of an approaching train, or roped to a log going over Niagara Falls, or handcuffed to a live bomb. She stopped the heartbeats of most moviegoers each week as—in the lurid words of a theater advertisement—"The villain perpetrates unbelievable evil tortures in his attempts to despoil Pauline's pure, unsullied body and force her to a fate worse than death."

A song, "Poor Pauline," highlighted the agonies of this unfortunate girl:

> *One night she's drifting out to sea,*
> *Then they tie her to a tree.*
> *I wonder what the end will be?*

Each week Pauline escaped, and each week "They" put her in greater peril.

> *Bing! Bang! Biff!*
> *They throw her off a cliff,*
> *They dynamite her in a submarine.*
> *In the lion's den she stands with fright,*
> *Lion goes to take a bite,*
> *Poor Pauline.*

Pearl emerged unscathed after nineteen jeopardy-filled episodes, each ending with a sudden "Continued Next Week," and soon afterward she started all over again. In *The Exploits of Elaine,* Pearl portrayed a heroine barely distinguishable from Pauline. By using extreme inventiveness, the producing company lengthened out Elaine's exploits to thirty-six weeks.

Blanche appeared in many, and her friendship with Pearl lengthened, too.

W. Christy Cabanne, an urbane and usually affable director, was casting one of the inevitable society dramas of the day and, looking through the extras, chose Blanche to play a tipsy debutante. That was how she expected it to happen: once discovered, you were on a speedway to stardom.

Wearing a sequined evening dress, she was to stagger past a gentleman seated at a restaurant table, stealthily pick up his cup (in which alcoholic drinks were hidden, to thwart prohibition authorities), gulp the contents, react, saying into camera (title to be inserted later), "Holy cow! It really is tea!" then slump to the floor and pass out.

Arc lights flared; the camera whirred.

It occurred to her that she could add something more, so while falling, she pulled the tablecloth down, too. Cups, plates, food and utensils spilled over her. The surprised actor whose drink she purloined fell off his chair and landed beside her.

Director Cabanne called "Cut!" loudly. Onlookers—including the crew—were laughing. Blanche jumped to her feet, expecting praise for her inventiveness.

"Was that an accident?" asked the director.

"No. I knew it would get a laugh."

He told the crew he would reshoot the scene. An annoyed wardrobe woman, eyeing Blanche's dress, said she would need a day to clean it.

"Don't bother," snapped Cabanne. "I'll use someone else. And when I need a co-director, Miss Ross, I'll let you know."

As she was walked off the set, a well-dressed visitor fell into step with her and said, with an Oxford accent, "He was quite wrong. You shouldn't be upset; you're a good actress."

"I'm not upset. I know I'm good."

She changed her clothes, and he drove her back to Manhattan in a snorting Stutz Bearcat, the sleek eye-catching motor car of the young and overprivileged. Prince J'Ali Ledene's car caught more eyes than most; it was pink.

A mercurial playboy, J'Ali was the descendant of an Egyptian viceroy. He was visiting the United States to study motion picture production and help develop that industry in Egypt. But within a few days of meeting Blanche, he began living only for her happiness. His was instant worship, punctuated with flowers, candy and compliments. No other admirer could match the way he pampered her. His eyes followed her every move; his words, soft and honeyed, proved irresistible, and they were soon involved in a passionate affair.

He was different. His mannerisms were a large part of his attractiveness, for physically, Blanche had to admit, J'Ali was no bargain. He was only of medium height, and insisted she wear low-heeled slippers so he would appear taller. He had red-blond hair which she playfully suggested was dyed, but he became angry at the insinuation and the subject was never discussed again. Friends noticed that J'Ali was the first of Blanche's lovers to make her submit absolutely to him, but as time would prove, he was also the last.

He was autocratic, firm, egotistic and neurotic. He wore gloves more often than not, never passed a faucet without washing his hands or a mirror without stopping to look into it. He placed a handkerchief over a doorknob before turning it and over a telephone mouthpiece before speaking into it.

His language was excessively flowery. His usual salutation to Blanche was "My angel of angels." He spent money lavishly, tried to make love in public, and aroused sharp antagonisms from her friends. J'Ali shrugged them off. He told her the men who had lost her to him were annoyed and the women who lost him to her were envious.

A cast-off showgirl warned Blanche that his heart was untouchable, his affection spurious, his visit to America a "fling," and when it was over Blanche would be flung to the winds. But when it was time for him to go home, he was as unhappy to leave as she was to see him go. It had developed into an emotional attachment stronger than both had intended it to be.

On their last night, he said, "I would like you to star in our films."

He described the tumultuous greeting he would arrange for her. She would be a queen in a nation that historically conferred majesty on beautiful women. She would have a barge of her own, and between pictures they would sail the Nile together.

To Blanche, a barge conjured up the clumsy flat-bottoms on the rivers around Manhattan, smelling of garbage. But J'Ali's barge meant a yacht laden with rapturous delights, one that would carry them "into Paradise on a river of perfume and incense."

Blanche was toying with the idea of going to Hollywood, the happy hunting ground for movie aspirants, but J'Ali was against it. He would provide a contract for her to star in his films immediately on his arrival in Cairo.

In the void created by his departure, it made a marvelous conversation piece. Should she go to Egypt or shouldn't she? There were doubters, pointing out the mysteries surrounding the subservience of women there—how would a female rebel cope with that? Others, even more skeptical, maintained that J'Ali's promise of Arabian nights was mere fantasy.

Each newly docked liner brought a flood of emotional outpourings but no contract. Political problems were holding up everything, he wrote, but he had powerful influence close to the throne and their difficulties would soon melt away.

The showgirl who had predicted he would dissolve into nothingness gloated, but Blanche was positive he would send for her. His letters continued to swear eternal love: "I have bumped my head on heaven and will never be the same."

To Pearl White, she read this excerpt: "Each night, I stand naked at my open window, facing west, my arms stretched out to you. Angel of angels, do the same toward me and it will be so that our hands will touch and we will be close to each other."

"It will be so that we'll both come down with pneumonia," she said wryly.

Pearl, the romanticist, thought it beautiful.

That summer, Blanche went to a rendezvous with J'Ali, but it was not his doing that made it possible. It came about partly because of the diminishing superstardom of Pearl White.

Like many early-day film actresses, Pearl gibberished when interviewed about herself. Her imagery contradicted so much

9

that not even the most reliable biographer could verify where she was born or when. She claimed, "I was a red-haired, cat-eyed brat who came from a tragic-minded family. One brother shot and killed himself with a shotgun; another was killed playing baseball. I wanted to be a circus bareback rider, then a writer, then a great dramatic actress, then a farm wife with a lot of children. I never got to be any of those."

But she didn't play those games with Blanche, with whom she was frank and unsophisticated. When Pathe Films billed her as "peerless and fearless," she said, "And petrified!"

She took risks, and had mishaps that never showed in her movies. They exacted a toll of continued pain. Of all her escapes, she wanted most to escape the action serials. Finally, she prevailed on producers at Fox Films to star her in dramatic roles.

The change in style was disastrous. Her army of fans deserted. The producers tried another feature-length drama, hoping to lure them back with a typical Pearl White title, *Without Fear*. But that didn't work either.

Then Pearl voluntarily canceled her contract with Fox and went back to Pathe, producers of her greatest successes. She agreed to another serial. This one, in fifteen episodes, was called *Plunder*. It was her last, her poorest and her most catastrophic.

A scene called for her to perch on top of a bus careening down a city street, then grab onto an overhead bridge and escape the villain—temporarily. Publicity men constantly played on the theme that Pearl White never used a double. But she was hurting badly and agreed to let a stuntman, John Stevenson, substitute for her. He missed the overhanging girder, fell to the pavement, and was killed. Shocked New Yorkers, watching the movie in the making, saw the accident and spread the word that she always shammed the dangerous stunts.

That night Pearl drank a lot, and Blanche sat around with her, drinking and smoking. It wasn't possible to keep Pearl's mind off what had happened.

"Y'know, I thought of asking you if you wanted to do that stunt. I'd have made them pay you a potful."

"After J'Ali left, I wondered if I could stand in for you. Then I decided standing in would wreck my chance to prove I'm a real actress."

"So you would have said 'No'?"

"Right you are."

To cap this pyramid of misery, Pearl's marriage to Wallace McCutcheon, her second matrimonial misadventure, was at an end. She felt lost. Behind the fearless façade of Pearl-Pauline-Elaine was a scared, insecure girl.

"Pearl was jinxed" was how Blanche saw this. "And it wasn't a happy time for me, either."

She was getting expressions of love from J'Ali, but that was all. The realist in her concluded he couldn't deliver his movie promises. "He's a Gemini," she said. "He thinks he means what he says. I wouldn't be a Gemini if they paid me!"

The old serials were running in postwar Europe, and Pearl still retained a glow of popularity there. She had offers to make movies in France and personal appearances in English music halls. "Why don't we get the hell out of here?" she asked. She accepted a contract from a French producer who proffered first-class transportation and hotel accommodations for two.

"It was an escape. We were running away," recalled Blanche. "But I was also running *to!*"

She cabled J'Ali that she was en route to Paris. The S.S. *Savoie* had barely cleared New York harbor when she received a wireless message that he would meet her there.

Their tickets were round-trip, and both girls expected to be back in three months. Neither one ever used the return half.

"Until you've lived a lot,
And loved a lot, and lost a lot,
You don't know Paree."
—Cole Porter

Pearl had been to Europe, and some recollections of that excursion were bittersweet. . . .

From a deck chair: "I'll tell you how suddenly I made up my mind that first time I went abroad. It was the Fourth of July, and I had a date to go to Coney Island. I broke the date and went to Paris. The whole thing was sudden. I never regretted it, but when I got back I heard the guy killed himself."

Some of her memories were myopic. . . .

She pictured the French capital as a dream city where enchanting adventures waited on every boulevard. She spiced her anecdotes with the flavor of money and music and perfume, mink and sables, diamonds and gold; extravagance was the way of life, everybody was rich. "But, of course," she admitted, "I didn't know a living soul."

Some of her adventures were bizarre. . . .

Her American passport gained her entrance into a private gambling casino where she watched players at roulette, won money for a stranger who kept asking her which number he should play.

He quit when he was $18,000 ahead and gave her half. She left the casino hurriedly, sure he would be after her. But she saw him only once, several days later, when she accidentally bumped into him. "He didn't even recognize me," she said. "That made me sore."

Each morning, as the *Savoie* plowed across the Atlantic, Blanche went to the wall map hanging in the salon. A movable arrow indicated the ship's position as it closed in on the coast of France. That, combined with Pearl's piquant stories, made her feel she was on the threshold of a new and exciting life.

13

And, at last, she was in Paris, alighting from the taxi at the Hôtel Claridge. The assistant manager greeted them as they came into the lobby. He had a small black mustache and matching hair brushed back over his forehead. He wore a grey pin-striped cutaway coat and baggy trousers. He walked slightly flat-footed.

He made a precise bow and said, "*S'il vous plaît*," and they followed him to the lift.

To reach it, they passed a salon with an American bar, its flooring a few steps below the level of the rest of the lobby. Although it was midday, the room was crowded and noisy, with a three-piece orchestra hacking out an uproarious French tune and a singer giving it her all, with gestures.

Led by the assistant manager, they paraded through the third-floor corridor to a suite that fronted on the Champs-Elysées. He was pleased with the way Blanche squealed with delight at the view from her window. It was obvious to him that she meant it; joy was written on her face as she looked down to the boulevard. The bedlam of horn-tooting cars often bothered newly arrived guests, but it excited her.

He showed her how to draw the curtains and the bath, bypassing the bidet, although it caught her attention (it puzzled her—she had never seen one before). He explained how easy it was to summon the porter, maid and floor waiter with illustrated buttons. He put extra pride, politeness and finesse into his customary routine. He was glad that she listened with such interest; he wanted her to—very much.

Then he raced down the stairs to his desk. The lift was slow and he was anxious. Anxious and curious.

Their passports disclosed that they were actresses. The mature one was Pearl Fay White Sutherland McCutcheon, born in Missouri more than thirty years before. He rarely went to the movies—he didn't recognize her and the name meant nothing to him. There was a previous visa to France stamped in it. But none in the other. The vivacious one was Blanche Rubenstein, actress, twenty-five, born in New York City.

So she was Jewish! What eyes! What a figure! Youth with mischievousness, laughter with self-assurance, poise and se-

14

renity. He wondered if centuries of suffering gave the women of her race some inner sublimity, as though in triumph over their tormentors. He was a student of history, and some day he hoped to find time to dwell on this. . . .

Soon afterward, Blanche heard a knock on the door.

He was returning her passport, staring at her, slack-jawed and motionless. Using her newly studied guidebook French, she said, "*Merci beaucoup*," and started to close the door.

"Pardon, mam'selle." His voice choked. "Look here, it is not my custom to do this, you will excuse . . . ?" He bowed. "My name is Claude Auzello. I observed"—he indicated her passport—"you have not been here before. I know Paris well. It is my city. That is to say, I was not born here, you understand, but I know it well. What I am saying, what I wish, is that you allow one who knows Paris well like myself to show this city to you! It would be my pleasure!"

She recognized the stare. Here she was in Paris less than an hour and already a conquest. It wasn't so different from New York after all.

"You're very kind," she said, "but I'm going to be busy. My time is taken." The look of regret in his eyes was too noticeable to be ignored, so she added, "I appreciate your offer very much."

Next morning, she had a cable from J'Ali that his arrival was delayed ten days.

Claude Auzello glowed when she told him she would be free after all and would like to have him show her his Paris.

That called for time off from work. He could have played sick or lied, but he was an extremely direct sort. Characteristically, he went to the hotel's Managing Directeur, Monsieur Arletty, who would understand.

He was lucky, he thought, that Monsieur Marquet was out of town. Marquet was a tough one; he owned the Claridge, the Métropole in Brussels, and the Casino at Ostend. He didn't employ Claude to play Paris guide for the guests; Marquet would have said "No."

He was the one who had lectured Claude when he first came

15

to the Claridge, warning him its empty rooms and beds were not there as handy shortcuts to sexual enjoyment.

But then it had happened. A girl was alone in the hotel—a White Russian refugee who had found sanctuary in France and still hoped that Russia's Communist government would topple.

She smiled and was charming whenever she saw Claude in the lobby. Her invitation was obvious, and he went to her room one night.

The next day he was summoned to Arletty's office and was shocked to learn she owed a large bill and had just informed the cashier that Claude would take care of it. He tried desperately to explain he didn't have that much money and hadn't had any idea of her situation. Arletty handled it with the finesse a good hotel man is supposed to have, and the woman checked out. Nothing was said to M. Marquet.

"She spoke nicely of you," Arletty told Claude. "She said you looked ferocious, but you were very, very sweet."

After that, he remained rigidly on guard against any misstep that could come about through proximity to double beds and single females.

As for Blanche, she played a guarded role in divulging information about herself and made no mention of J'Ali. After the first day of their tour, she informed Pearl that she found Claude an attractive escort and looked forward to seeing him the rest of the week. But she wouldn't share any secrets or engage in any intimacies. Theirs was to be a brief acquaintanceship, limited to an outside duration of ten days.

Because she volunteered so little, he thought her quite naïve. That was a quality he liked in girls. And when he didn't take her arm crossing the streets, it gave her a good feeling because he was letting her be herself. That was a quality she liked in men.

And she thought him naïve. It struck her that he looked young enough to be her brother but acted old enough to be her father. He seemed almost too thoughtful for a man not yet thirty. In addition to describing sights they were looking at, he often interspersed historical facts about them. Her American boyfriends didn't know who was buried in Grant's tomb and couldn't care less.

When they sat in a café, he asked if she wished coffee or tea; she took the tea but wished it were cognac. Once, noting his uneasiness, she literally pushed him into a pissoir that he was going to pass by despite his evident need. (An episode involving that need played an important part in his life, but he wasn't disposed to tell her about it then.)

They strolled the flower market and climbed to the top of the Eiffel Tower. He had an easy manner of selling her on the beauties of the city, and she enjoyed seeing his enjoyment. But she turned down a visit to the zoo at Vincennes. "I'd rather not," she said, explaining that schoolday tours of the Bronx Park Menagerie had provided her with all the education she desired on that subject.

She balked, too, at Notre-Dame and the Sacré-Coeur. "No churches. I don't go at home, so why should I here?"

"You joke?"

"No." She smiled and shook her head to accentuate her feelings. Later, he said, "It was the way she smiled when she said 'No' that won my heart so completely."

She followed him into a shrine on the Ile de la Cité that had to be seen only at this time of the afternoon when the sun was at a place in the sky where it showed dazzlingly through the red, gold and blue stained-glass window. It was beautiful and she was impressed.

When Pearl asked how she had enjoyed the day, she said, "I saw a toilet that you wouldn't believe. Just a hole in the ground with a place for your feet. Girls squat like Indians and balance themselves like acrobats!" But she admitted that Claude was the most interesting young man she had ever met and she would always remember him.

Claude reported to his associates in the hotel that a memorable moment had occurred at the Etoile. They stood at the curb of the Champs-Elysées, looking across at the Arc de Triomphe.

Suddenly Blanche said, "I want to touch it," and plunged

17

into a maelstrom of traffic, walking straight toward the monument. Claude was transfixed, unable to believe his eyes, then rushed after her, gained her side, and they continued across, while automobiles skidded and swirled and piled up, brakes grinding, tires squealing, horns tooting and drivers screaming obscenities.

"She was holding up her hand like a gendarme," he said. "Her hair was flying, her skirt whipping in the wind. It is a miracle that we are alive."

"You have no cause for worry," laughed an associate. "No French motorist will hit a long-legged American girl!"

The quaint byways of Montmartre delighted her, but she disavowed interest in museums. "Today I saw the Louvre," she informed Pearl. "I got out of there so fast we could have been ghosts." She enjoyed writing home on the postcards, "I've been haunting this place."

Across from the Louvre, she balked when he suggested they stroll through the gardens of the Palais-Royal.

"I'm a city person. All I know about flowers is that there are roses, orchids and violets and they grow in corsages."

"For me," he said, "a garden is a retreat when I have the inner agitation."

So she went. They watched silent couples strolling past, hand in hand, embracing without warning, kissing, sighing, gazing soulfully at each other.

"It's our nature to love." He gestured toward a couple whose bodies appeared permanently locked together. "Always, Parisians love love the best."

It sounded like a preamble to an invitation to bed.

She thought, "Here it comes," but it simply reminded him of another cherished discovery. He took her to a quai on the Left Bank where a long-ago Romeo had planted a pattern of cobblestones in the shape of a human heart. Blanche could imagine the delight of the maiden when she beheld this valentine, and when she told him so, it pleased him very much.

She, in turn, was pleased by his circumspect manners. "I like the way he keeps his distance," she told Pearl.

18

Claude, his head in the stars, telephoned his father in Nice. "I'm in love with a beautiful American girl. I want your permission to marry her."

"Why must you marry an American girl? We have millions of beautiful girls in France."

"None like her!"

"Then marry her immediately!"

The time to tell her was already fixed in his mind. It would be Sunday afternoon. He would take her to tea at the Ritz.

Hotels were his life, and wherever they went, he pointed them out to her, some with reverence, some with contempt, airing his knowledge of their histories, their splendor or lack of it. He knew them inside and out, not just in Paris—he had worked in them in various cities in Europe during summer vacations when he was a small boy.

If he could ever have one of his own, he knew where it would be, and as they strolled toward the Ritz he showed her. It was a four-floor residence on the Rue du Faubourg Saint-Honoré.

"Look how it goes through to the Avenue Gabriel, which is named for the architect of Louis the Fifteenth. From the top floor one sees the Tuileries and across the Place de la Concorde to the Seine. It will make an elegant and expensive hotel, ideal for Americans."

He had made inquiries, and the house was for sale, but the two sisters who owned it disliked each other, and when one mentioned a price, the other demanded more for her half. The impasse was in his favor, he said; it gave him time to try to raise money. But so far, he only had vague promises from bankers.

As they went on toward the Place Vendôme, he said, "I would like that you know that I am ambitious and will not remain an assistant manager forever."

The hotel he admired most was the one he pointed out when they had reached the Place Vendôme and stood beside the Napoleon monument.

"It is the creation of César Ritz," he said. "And look here, how his name is now a part of the language. You know, of course, he made it stand for elegance; it means deluxe and ultra-chic. I will tell you about him too some day."

They crossed to the door of the hotel, half-hidden in an alcove. Traffic moved languidly around the Vendôme, minimal movement on Sunday afternoon. A few pedestrians strolled by. The Claridge had a large electric sign over its monstrous entrance. But even on a busy midweek day, the unacquainted might pass the Ritz and never notice its *porte-cochère*.

César Ritz had bought and broken through walls of three private residences. They differed in height from two stories surrounding a *petit jardin* to three and four stories on the Place Vendôme, while the building over the north garden climbed to five and the building on the Rue Cambon side was six. Underground there was a massive kitchen, wine stocks, and storage space for trunks belonging to wandering guests.

There were sloping Mansard roofs. Beneath each notch were Mansard garrets and attic chambers, named after builder François Mansard. (Another Mansard, Jules, designed the palace at Versailles.) Below were galleries, pavilions and a profusion of flowers in beds and pots. From opening day, June 1, 1898, the world's famous were drawn to the two hundred ten rooms and apartments that comprised César Ritz's hotel.

Until then, every hotel had only one bathroom to a floor, but Ritz installed one in every apartment. (Oscar Wilde didn't approve. "Who wants to live with an unmovable wash basin? I will ring for water when I need it." And Ritz redesigned the toilet seats because England's King Edward VII didn't like their shape.) A Swiss clock, chic and silent, adorned each bedroom, which also contained big brass beds with horsehair mattresses and white China chamber pots beneath. Guests who brought their own servants could have them linked to their quarters with a private push button.

The Royal Suite's first occupant was the King of Sweden, its second the Prince of Wales, that famed boulevardier who became Edward VII. King Leopold of Belgium, King Carol,

Queen Marie, and Magda Lupescu of Romania slept in the Royal Suite, and when the Grand Duke Nicholas of Russia was there, the entire hotel was ringed by guards, to see to his safety. "Look here, how important it is for guests to be secure," Claude told Blanche.

But every great hotel, he noted, must be prepared to cope with death, and it was no stranger to the Ritz.

In 1915, René Ritz, youngest of the founder's two sons, jumped down an elevator shaft after being rejected by the army. It was a drawn-out suicide: he cracked his spine and lingered three years in agony. So rarely was this horror mentioned by family or personnel that it was commonly believed he had succumbed to spinal meningitis.

In October 1918, soon after René died, César Ritz passed away in a private hospital in Kussnacht, Switzerland, where he had been confined in a mindless condition for six years. To Claude, he was immortal, the hotel his monument.

It was evident to Blanche that the welfare of a hotel he esteemed was a personal matter to Claude. "It is true," he said, "that the troubles at the Ritz have never come from its royal guests. No assassinations, no murders, no suicides, no robberies, no scandals. That is a record to admire, I say."

He had less admiration for theatrical royalty. The Ritz had reason, he felt, to turn away luminaries of the stage and screen. In 1920, actress Olive Thomas died at the hotel, the manner of her death cloaked in secrecy.

She was on her honeymoon with Jack Pickford, high-strung, high-flying brother of "America's Sweetheart." Gossip columnists reported that she had married as a reflex action to a tempestuous affair with Florenz Ziegfeld, Jr., in whose "Follies" she had appeared before her movie career. The hotel refused to admit the truth of a rumor that she leaped from her window and landed on the terrace near where her husband was seated.

The silence compounded the mystery-drama, already loaded with elements so beloved by journalists. Glamour, sex, tragedy.

"Was it suicide?" asked the newspapers in bold-faced type.

21

Had she taken drugs? Was it deliberate or accidental? One lurid Paris magazine offered the theory, almost hopefully, that her husband had poisoned her.

Claude approved of the hotel's decision to say nothing.

The police investigation was hurried and inconclusive. The body was cremated without an autopsy. "It is imperative that a hotel like the Ritz maintain close relations with the police," said Claude, who doubted that influence was used to circumvent evidence of poison. The death of Olive Thomas passed into history as unobtrusively as the hotel could manage, a rather difficult feat considering all that was involved. She was only twenty-two.

It was comparatively simple to get away from the gloomy anecdotes of death when he guided Blanche through the *galerie* leading to the Rue Cambon. It was studded with showcases glittering with wares from the finest shops.

"I am in the employ of the Claridge," he said, "and it is not in me to be disloyal, but the distinction between these two . . . you see for yourself."

Indeed she could. The Claridge lobby jumped with garish sounds day and night, many filtering in from the never-sleeping Champs-Elysées. The hotel's rear doors were on the Rue de Ponthieu, a thoroughfare laced with cabarets that exploded with activities from dark to dawn. Girls stood invitingly on every corner, boisterous tourists promenaded endlessly, males, young and old, sailed up and down in their restless hunt for amusement, while, over all, *Le Jazz Hot* blared from the clubs, and predatory doormen beckoned every passerby to partake of the special pleasures to be found inside.

The Ritz was quiet, dignified, respectable, scented with the heady perfume of money. It had an air of being a supreme aristocrat, while the Claridge, by comparison, was a soubrette at the Opéra-Comique.

Later, Blanche said, "I knew the minute I saw the Ritz, *that* was for me!"

They sat on the terrace, out of the center and apart from the correctly dressed clientele and the rustle of laughter and conversation.

She knew he was going to get around to a proposal by his nervousness, the way he dropped the phrase "Someday I will tell you more about this . . ." into many descriptions.

He wanted to tell her about the Napoleon Monument and his admiration for the Emperor, but she stopped him. She told Pearl later: "I heard myself saying, much to my surprise, 'I would rather hear about you!'"

The education of Claude Auzello was an extensive one; it included schooling in three countries, the mastery of five languages, and the rigors of military training.

He was born in Monte Carlo, where his father's market catered to the Royal Palace and "*le beau gentil*" of that select little principality. An uncle ran a resort hotel at Cap Menton, and other relatives were in the cork industry that flourished on Sardinia. Claude sampled both vocations before deciding he would be a lawyer.

He attended Jansen de Saille in Paris, passed the bar examination, and was handed his diploma just as France was handing a declaration of war to the Kaiser of Germany.

Assigned to the artillery, he became celebrated on his sector of the western front for an action that was only peripherally related to the movements of the French and German armies.

He manned a solitary command post, dangerously close to the enemy, connected by telephone to the gunners behind the lines, his duty being to observe enemy movements and direct the cannon firing against them.

One day, he related, "I was seized by an uncontrollable but natural desire. I told the officer on the other end of the phone I would make my way to a nearby wood and return as soon as possible. He ordered me to stay where I was. 'Look here,' I said, 'I am damned if I will stink up this little box that I must exist in!' The officer shouted, 'You stay! This is an order!' I hung up and wiggled my way into the trees to relieve myself. Suddenly, the Boche let go a barrage. I saw the box blown to pieces by a direct hit. Even the phone was gone!"

The men behind the lines were sure he had been killed. The officer who had commanded him to stay at his post was overcome with remorse. When Claude showed up, unscathed, a celebration took place. Wine was drunk and speeches were made, praising him for saving his own life by obeying Nature's orders rather than those of the army. Actually, he distinguished himself well during the war. In fact, too well. The military became so attached to him that, instead of demobilizing him, it dispatched him to the Ruhr to head the troops policing defeated Germany's coal mines at Saarbrücken.

Finally discharged with a Legion of Honor, he discovered his law-school classmates had gained a substantial head start. The field was overcrowded. It was then that he opted for a career in hotels, a vocation that promised glamour, constant shifts of intrigue, a background for adventures by day and night, amid a changing cast of characters.

His recital of some of these details brought him back to the subject of love. Omitting the affair with the Russian refugee ("until later, you understand"), he said he had shown many attractive girls to their rooms in the hotels he worked in. "But," he said, "none like you." He confessed to her that he was trying hard to make her fall in love with Paris because he wanted her to stay, to make her life . . . He was about to add, "with me," but she interrupted.

"I like you, Claude," she said. "But you mustn't get ideas about us. I am not as free as you think. A man to whom I am very attached will be in Paris in a day or two, and when he arrives, I won't be seeing you anymore."

He said "No!" so vehemently that people turned their heads and the maître d' moved near and frowned. She kept silent. Then he settled the bill for their lunch, and they took a taxi back to the Claridge.

Crossing the pavement toward the hotel entrance, she stopped, pulled him toward her, and kissed him gently. He tried to press his body hard against hers, but she pushed him away and went on into the hotel, while he stayed there on the Champs-Elysées and watched her go.

3

"All that really counts is money!"
—Aristotle Socrates Onassis

J'Ali checked into the Claridge in a flurry of commotion, bringing a mountain of luggage, two manservants and a retinue of noisy companions.

Claude saw Blanche run across the lobby and embrace the new arrival. Hardly able to contain his emotion, he led the group upstairs, unlocked the door, threw wide the curtains, and waited to see if the suite met with approval.

J'Ali hardly glanced at the rooms, and not at all at the assistant manager. He was indifferent to the routine of satisfying newly arriving guests.

"I ordered everything disinfected before my arrival."

Claude consulted a memorandum. "It's been done," he said. J'Ali sniffed, shook his head. "I should detect it."

"The porter will have dissipated the odor."

"Send him to me; I'll see to it myself. Take away your towels and linen. I have my own. I require the waiters who serve me to wear gloves—clean white ones. Reserve a table for ten at Maxim's tonight at the dinner hour, then at Le Boeuf sur le Toit." His eyes lit on a bottle of champagne and a gift basket of fruit from the management. "Have those removed. I want a box for four in the Jockey Club Sunday at Longchamps."

Claude tried to catch Blanche's eye, but she was in conversation with two young Egyptians. He flared. "You should consider if your excellency would be happier elsewhere. Paris has many hotels that cater to special needs. Perhaps we are not equipped."

J'Ali took Blanche's arm. "The équipage of this hotel suits me better than anywhere else, Monsieur."

As he was going out, Blanche left the Prince's side and

25

caught up with Claude at the door. "I see now, I should have told you right at the beginning."

He followed them to Le Boeuf sur le Toit, on Rue Boissy d'Anglas. It was crowded, and Claude bitterly catalogued its habitués as drug addicts, alcoholics, wealthy idlers, pederasts and lesbians. It was founded by Jean Cocteau, himself an addict. There were members of the élite of Paris there— artists, poets, musicians—but Claude saw only the dregs. He sat at the bar, watched J'Ali introduce Blanche to Cocteau, and to film directors René Clair and Luis Buñuel, who were combining talents with Salvador Dali to make a surrealist film. She sat with Vincent de Noailles, who was given to financing films, and in Zelli's, in Montmartre, she engaged in extensive conversation with handsome Edmond Van Daele, a reigning film star, well built, with wavy black hair.

The cynical poet of the city, one-armed Blaise Cendrars, drunk at the bar, aired caustic reflections on the vagaries of Paris society, which Claude overheard, although Cendrars was addressing his comments to the companion who occupied the next stool, his dog.

During the next three days, Blanche and J'Ali drove through the Bois to sumptuous garden restaurants; J'Ali engaged in a polo match and spent hours with her at a school learning the Charleston, the new American dance introduced by Josephine Baker. This energetic display of acrobatics eclipsed the Apache Waltz, the Tango and the Bunny Hug; everybody in Paris was doing it.

Tiring of Le Boeuf sur le Toit, where throngs made dancing impossible, J'Ali took Blanche ringside at the Club Acacias, which featured Clifton Webb and the Dolly Sisters pirouetting in colorful Indonesian costumes, upturned shoes and precariously balanced pagoda-like headpieces. Then they alternated between the Acacias and the Jardin de Ma Soeur, where Maurice performed graceful ballroom steps with Eleanora Hughes. Each night, Claude followed them as closely as he dared, sometimes until dawn, never letting them see him. When they went back to the hotel, he forced himself to forgo his surveillance; the torment was unendurable.

26

Sunday mornings, the Prince played hard sets of tennis, then they motored to the races. Once—and Claude noticed and added it to his bitterness—their limousine whirled over the cobblestone heart but didn't slow down. Claude thought the wheels accelerated.

Blanche had told J'Ali about that paved heart, but she didn't know its location; the roadway on the Left Bank was entirely covered by cobblestones, and the Prince merely showed polite disinterest. He didn't care to see the sun shine through the stained glass windows of the Ile de la Cité church, or to stroll through the Jardin de Palais-Royal, either.

They attended the races with J'Ali's friend, a Prince Fahmi-Bey, and a lovely French widow, Marguerite Alibert Laurent, whom he planned to marry. Fahmi was a carbon copy of J'Ali in that he was in fierce pursuit of pleasure and had all the time in the world for it. He used the same flowery language with Marguerite that Blanche heard from the Prince. Younger than J'Ali, he more than matched him in eccentricities, but Blanche would learn about those later, when she and Marguerite could converse properly, for at the time of their first meeting, Blanche had little grasp of French and Marguerite did not speak English.

Fahmi's family had secured a position for him as an attaché with the Egyptian legation in London. It was hardly more than an honorary position, though it entitled him to the lavish bounties accorded members of the diplomatic corps; he was not looking forward to England. He had no need for bounties. He wanted Egypt, where he subsisted on an income of a half-million dollars a year and kept a racing car and four Rolls-Royces.

He envied J'Ali's upcoming return to their homeland, and conversation about Egypt occupied them all one afternoon, for J'Ali was more determined than ever to get Blanche to go there with him. The film contract was still stalled, but he promised it would be finalized soon after he got back to Cairo.

Checking space that would be available in the week ahead, Claude saw that Blanche and J'Ali were vacating their rooms. He kept a watch for her and then said, "You are leaving?"

"Yes."

"I want to see you on an urgent matter."

"I'll be in Paris again."

"You are going far?"

"To Egypt."

Monsieur Marquet was in the hotel, saw them together, and summoned him. Despondently, he left her and reported to the hotel owner. Like many in the higher echelon, Marquet was aware of Claude's infatuation. He gave him a strong lecture against any liaison with guests, and a warning not to neglect his duties.

Claude walked out while Marquet was still speaking.

He went straight upstairs and rushed into J'Ali's suite. Shaking his fist at the astounded Prince, he shouted, "See here, if you take Blanche to Egypt it will turn her into an international tramp. She will be finished! I see it clearly. In the eyes of society she will be just a cheap whore—and all because of you!"

As J'Ali stood speechless, Claude went on, "You cannot take her! I love her! I want to marry her! I will make a good life for her. . . ."

J'Ali called the two Egyptian servants.

"Put him out!" he commanded. "He's crazy!" They pushed Claude into the hall and slammed the door.

Blanche heard J'Ali's version when she came in. He wanted to know, "Who is this madman and what is he to you?"

She said, "I told you about him. He showed me around Paris."

They went to the lobby together, the outraged Prince sweeping past Claude's desk, calling for the manager. Blanche stopped and said, "How dare you talk to the Prince about me?"

"It is true, what I said."

"You had no right to go to him. I live my own life. Perhaps this will convince you."

She gave him a hard slap. It was like a gunshot, and the sound froze everyone within hearing.

"Oh, Claude!" she exclaimed. "My God! Why did I do that? I didn't mean to! I didn't! I didn't!"

She tried to blink back tears and failed and let him take her in his arms.

J'Ali emerged with M. Marquet from the latter's office to see Blanche in Claude's embrace. He was dumfounded; right from the beginning he had refused to let her have any contacts with other men. Claude gazed at him pugnaciously, but J'Ali's fury was with Blanche. He turned his back and stalked away. She brushed Claude's cheek with another kiss and said, "Thank you. Thank you. Thank you, thank you."

Then Claude looked at Marquet. The big boss smiled encouragement at him, then glanced at the receding back of J'Ali and laughed.

"Claude thinks I'm in love with him," she told Pearl later that same day. "But it's just that I didn't mean to slap him and I felt sorry for him."

J'Ali came into her room not long after that, prepared to forgive. He brought a leather and gold embossed Koran and wanted her to swear she would never see Claude again. She refused.

"You are marrying this room clerk?"

"If I do, he won't be a room clerk long, believe me."

On Sunday, she suggested to Claude that he take her back to the Ritz, and if he still felt the same way, he should finish the sentence she had interrupted the previous time.

He did, and this time she accepted him.

Before leaving, J'Ali asked for a lock of her hair, and Blanche snipped off a fragment. She watched him place it inside a silver locket, to be worn, he said, "within sound of the beating of my heart through eternity!"

Jubilantly, Claude telephoned his father in Nice, to let him be the first to know he was going to marry his "American," while she wrote her family in New York that she was engaged to a "wonderful Frenchman."

It was important to Claude that she go south with him. "I could not marry until my father sees you."

Before the trip could be arranged, she received an offer to

play in a film opposite Edmond Van Daele. Her role in *La Lumière du Coeur* would be larger than any parts she had played at home.

It meant postponement of all Claude's plans.

She apologized. "I got excited, I guess, because it's not just one picture. They want a contract for two more—if this one turns out good. After all, I am an actress."

He begged her to consult him about these changing events in her life.

"I shall be the one who decides," he told her.

"We'll see," she said. "Probably."

When the film was completed, it was booked into the Théâtre Ponthieu, adjacent to the rear entrance of the hotel.

Claude sneaked off to the matinee as often as he could, especially timing his presence to her big scene, when she fought off Van Daele's embrace and nearly finished him with a convenient mallet close at hand. At the conclusion of this imbroglio, Claude always hurried back to his desk, without waiting to see her reconciliation and final kiss with the film star.

Van Daele exercised his option on her for another film, and although Claude showed pride in his actress-fiancée, he was unhappy because it meant further delay.

It was apparent to his friends that he was going to have his hands full with his "American." They thought her opinionated and spoiled, openly deriding French codes of behavior. She would never be obedient to him, they warned, or acknowledge her husband as master, as French wives were expected to do.

Blanche knew they considered her attitude toward religion "unsaintly," her profanity unwomanly. She spoke openly of sex instead of treating it as an intimate subject. "Hell," she said one night, "you all do it—what's so damn secret about it?" But her husband-to-be still kept hands off.

Her films with Van Daele were only so-so successes, and she confessed to Claude that although it hurt to say so, she was having doubts about her acting ability. "Maybe I'm not as good as I think I am."

He took a leave of absence from the hotel, mapped out their

route, and arranged to drive south in a borrowed monster of a car, an Hispano-Suiza.

He was a careful driver, and they motored leisurely past Fontainebleau, Sens and Avallon to the Hôtel de la Poste at Saulieu for lunch. He knew the history of every mile they traveled.

Late that afternoon they crossed the Rhone at Vienne to the Hôtel Beau-Rivage at Condrieu, where he had reserved rooms. It was an intimate little chalet. There were only a handful of other guests. Winter weather lingered.

She saw the manager behind the desk take up two keys before he started to escort them upstairs.

"Two rooms?" she asked. Then she looked at Claude.

"We're not children. Let's act our age."

The hotel man nodded agreeably and changed the two keys for one.

"This room is more comfortable," he said. "And the bed, too."

The Rhone, inspiration of painters and lovers, surged below the hotel terrace. He canceled their reservations ahead, and they stayed nearly a week. She slept with him and he was happy.

Now she knew Paris was her destined home. It had become a love affair between a girl of twenty-six and a city of two thousand years. Claude had made her fall in love with Paris; it was now his problem to make her fall in love with him.

Nights at Condrieu forced him to change his schedule. They barreled down to the Riviera, bypassing the exquisite places he had planned for her to see. They would have very little time with his family. In Nice, at the Villa Linda, home of Joseph and Melinda Auzello, they were sedately separated. Blanche had a small room on the third floor. The air was heavy with the aroma of oranges, lilacs and mimosa. She slept at the top of the bright yellow house; he slept in the room below, where his father slept, too. Lovemaking dwelled in their hearts, but the stairs were narrow and they creaked and kept them apart.

Blanche gave full vent to her soaring spirits. Claude's father was enchanted with her. Claude's mother, fanatically Catholic, was considerably less so. Relatives from Menton, Monaco and Corsica flocked in to see the "American." Joseph met them all at the door and advised them that Claude had found an ideal mate and he had given his parental blessing for the union. That forestalled questions. With a sideways swipe at his dour wife, he said, "Blanche provides him with the laughing misery of love." So no one mentioned religion. Instead, they spoke of hotels, and Blanche said, "I won't be happy until Claude is running the Ritz."

Some considered it arrogant, but later thought it memorable.

They were married at eleven in the morning at the Hôtel de Ville, City Hall of Paris, with Blanche's mother in from New York to attend. Joseph came up from Nice. They were the witnesses; there were no others.

Reporting on the serene tempo of their wedding day, the Paris *Herald* ran a weather report surely calculated to promise true happiness for a bride:

> The brief wintry spell is at an end and the agreeable mildness of Spring has returned to the satisfaction of all Parisians. The warm sunshine should tempt families into the parks and gardens during the afternoon.

Instead of being tempted into a park or garden, the new husband left his bride immediately after the ceremony and rushed back to the Claridge to finish routine work before their departure for a Brussels honeymoon. Blanche was outraged; it was her first intimation of how formidable this rival would be.

"If you love the damn hotel more than you do me, don't let me come between you," she said. She locked him out of the nuptial suite he had booked after she refused to take a late train to Brussels. He couldn't raise a fuss in the hotel where he was assistant manager. How could he face the staff? He slept in a small hotel, the Lincoln, on the Rue Bayard. No one knew him there.

Next day, the newspaper reported:

Yesterday's temperature failed to reach its expected warmth. Most people found the sunny side of the street preferable.

"You are foolish to say I love the hotel more," he told her when she came downstairs next morning.

He reminded her that his friends waited to entertain them in Brussels.

They dashed for the noon train.

Van Daele, Pearl White and others from her film world came with magnums of champagne to see them off. They whooped it up until the wheels began to roll. Then the celebrants gulped the wine and shattered their glasses and followed Pearl, screaming, onto the platform.

The train was barely out of the terminal before Claude spoke up, very earnestly.

"Look here, on the day of his marriage to Josephine Beauharnais, Napoleon wrote to a woman who had been a witness to their wedding that she was no longer a proper person to associate with his wife."

Blanche stared at him.

"Darling, I'm not Josephine."

"But you will give up these people?"

"No. Of course I won't."

They moved apart, and she opened a makeup kit and refreshed her lip rouge.

"Look here," he said, "you're to stop using this."

She had been joking with Pearl about the marriage license and had hung it in the train cabin. She gestured toward it.

"Is that our marriage certificate or a declaration of war?"

"You have natural color, Blanchette," he pleaded. "It is enough."

"I've been using rouge since I was sixteen." She thought it over, then corrected it. "Thirteen."

"Look here, you are now Madame Auzello. I find you beautiful, so it is finished."

Her makeup box was a large one. He picked it up and hurled it out the window of the moving train.

At the next station she ran to the door of the car and leaped off. There was a Paris-bound train on a neighboring track. The furious bride boarded it and was immediately carried back toward their starting point, while her amazed groom, finally emerging from his state of shock, reached the platform just in time to see a train with his bride disappear in one direction, as their luggage was carried off in another.

Hours later, he dashed into the Paris terminal. She was sitting quietly on a bench waiting for him. He kissed her tenderly on her newly rouged lips. Their first marital skirmish was over.

There was no other train to Brussels that day. To explain why they had returned so precipitately, they contrived a story that Blanche, unused to the quiet departures of the French railway trains, had stepped onto a way-station platform to buy sandwiches and the train took off for Brussels without her. It was plausible—it pictured a wildly distraught bridegroom and a lost bride. It struck the risibilities of their friends and was told and retold around Paris, where, for years, they would be pointed out as the newlyweds to whom it had happened.

Claude's first impression of this American had been of a stunning creature of style and brilliance. Now he discovered she had an easy going approach to morals and was used to more money than she or he had ever known. Yet he saw this pinnacle of femininity as worth storming, that they could make a beautiful pairing of male and female, one that might lead to heights even beyond those either of them had ever dreamed they could aspire to.

For this ideal, he discarded celibacy and embraced marriage. It would lead to a mismatched, almost incomprehensible union of two people from two unrelated worlds, utterly unsuited to each other in tastes, preferences and beliefs.

They rented an apartment in Passy, beside the Seine, where Claude swiftly learned there was an important subject he had never discussed. His Blanchette couldn't cook.

"I don't know how to light the stove," she told him. "I'm willing to learn if you're willing to wait."

A young widow with a two-year-old daughter was engaged. Elise Mazaye knew her way around a kitchen stove.

The law of France expressly stated the husband was master and controlled the household (including his wife), but Claude had an uncomfortable feeling the law wasn't being observed in his home.

She was outspoken against the French Civil Code and the way it slanted life in favor of the male. As if that wasn't bad enough, she expressed her opinion to his friends. Outraged, he stalked out of the apartment and stayed away until after midnight. Returning, he expected to find her contrite, ready to submit to his wishes on how their marriage should continue. She was sitting up in a bed littered with copies of the Paris editions of the *New York Herald* and the *Chicago Tribune* turned to the sports pages. She said brightly, "The Yanks have won again," and turned out the lights.

Often, she waited for him in the lobby with guests he had introduced to her. Sometimes she made friends with them, but once he returned to find annoyed silence from the assemblage. And in their presence she told him, "I can't stand bores and you can't make me!"

Claude was appalled—righteously, in a hotel man's view— because two of the guests checked out earlier than they had said they would.

Two months after their marriage, Arletty left the hotel and Marquet offered Claude the post of manager. The promotion should have sparked jubilation in the newlyweds, but they were dissatisfied because Marquet refused to give him a contract. While they debated, Blanche saw the name of Otto H. Kahn, American banker and philanthropist, in a Paris newspaper. He was at the Crillon, not far from the property Claude coveted for a hotel of his own.

They went to see him and found him receptive. If Claude would invest his own money, Kahn would add to it. Also, he would bring in others. The two sisters who owned the property agreed on a price and the cost of an option. Exultant, Claude decided to risk his savings; Blanche enthusiastically agreed.

But government permissions were needed. The Bureau of Licenses opposed a hotel on that site because it would be only a pistol shot from the Elysées Palace, where the head of state resided. That individual could see no reason for a hotel in such proximity and was dead set against pistol shots.

While he made desperate attempts to get the permits approved, Claude received an offer to become assistant manager of the Ritz.

It was a unique opportunity. Employees there didn't often start so high, but the widow of César Ritz required someone at once. Marie Louise, who made the offer, was a capable successor to her husband, despite problems confronting members of her sex in dominant positions. To offset these, she had two male executives up front with her. They were Victor Rey and Hans Pfyffer, in both of whom she placed enormous confidence.

Blanche favored immediate acceptance. Claude could gauge the extent of her enthusiasm by her promise to get along on his salary.

He was eager to please her, but taking the job at the Ritz meant dropping the fight for the Saint-Honoré property. If he fought on, he might yet get the permit, but it would take time. It was a difficult decision to make, especially for a cautious fellow such as himself. He and Blanche strolled in the Gardens of the Palais-Royal to reflect on it.

There was one bright spot, in his estimation. The offer from Madame Ritz provided him with leverage he could use to gain the contract he wanted from the owner of the Claridge.

She frowned at the thought he would continue there.

"Look here, Blanchette. I admire César Ritz, as you know. But his ideals are being lost. Old clients are turning to other hotels. I could show Madame Ritz how to proceed, but not as an assistant manager. It is a position without power."

She thought that could be solved easily. "Tell her to make you manager and you'll fix things."

He kept an appointment with Marie Louise, while Blanche sat waiting for him in the lobby on the Vendôme side. She was turned away from the Petit Bar, where ladies—even with escorts—were not allowed.

There was pageantry to be observed while she waited, but not to such drumming sounds of jazz as thumped through the Claridge. Music at the Ritz came from a string trio sprinkling the air with a mingling of schmaltz con pizzicato.

Passing toward the elevators and the *galerie* were clusters of stylish young people, fashionable middle-aged, sharp-looking military men in blue. And, too, quaint relics of the nobility uprooted by the 1914–1918 war—titled old men and women, lurching, staggering, drifting by her, conjuring up images of half-sunk galleons, neither on top or bottom of the seas, drifting with the currents, bumping into one another. Or they stood in clumps like gnarled oaks, leaning stiffly as if against a strong wind.

The music from the terrace was often blanketed by a babel of foreign tongues, a mixture of the languages of Europe and the Americas, the incomprehensible of the Middle East and the indistinguishable of Asia. Blanche was acquiring a rudimentary knowledge of French and retained excellent command of German because of painstaking efforts by her parents to drive it into her.

A group of opulent Germans surged toward the elevator, their attention centered on a lady who had just checked in and was being shown upstairs to her room. She was dripping strings of pearls down her bosom.

Blanche heard a fragment of her conversation, in German, as she passed.

"Ah, yes," she was saying. "We always come to this hotel because they don't take Jews!"

At that moment, Claude came leaping down the stairs, ran up to her, and said, "Madame, tonight you sleep with the manager of the Ritz Hotel!"

4

"Fish, like human beings, are not infallible and may make a mistake during prolonged activity."
—Charles Ritz, A FLY FISHER'S LIFE

Blanche scanned the daily guest register of the Ritz. "This reminds me of how my mother used to read the death notices religiously. She just looked for Jewish names."

The register included an Arabian sheik with an entourage of twenty ("No Jews there, I bet"), the Brazilian Ambassador ("Do they have any there?"), Nancy Cunard, Marquise Cassati ("A maid told me she keeps a snake in her room—a real snake, not the two-legged kind"), Gabrielle "Coco" Chanel ("There's a lady I'd like to meet; we have a lot in common"), Joseph Duveen, Calouste Gulbenkian, Dudley Field Malone, Lord and Lady Mountbatten ("In the honeymoon suite—do you have to prove you're married?"), the Duchess of Talleyrand-Périgord, . . .

Claude wanted to know how she had secured the list.

She didn't remember. The hotel employed four hundred workers, and she was making friends with them all. One of them gave it to her. The indiscretion appalled him.

"See here," he said, "this list is confidential. You'll get some fellow in hot water, and it will go badly for me, too. There are people who do not want me as the manager."

She showed disbelief at that. He went on to explain that his appointment was contrary to the training routine inaugurated by César Ritz.

New young employees began as kitchen helpers. After six months of peeling potatoes (carefully), and washing and stacking dishes (quietly), the newcomer was moved to the lobby to open doors (courteously) or to a dining room to be a busboy (invisibly) and then serve for at least a year as a waiter (artistically). Artist-writer Ludwig Bemelmans, who had Ritz training on the lower rungs of the ladder, wrote, "Before departing, I learned how to press a duck, open a bottle and push a chair under a lady." Claude offered a son of American hotel tycoon Conrad Hilton a training course, and the youth began his first day with potato-peeling in the kitchen. He never showed up for the second day of the course.

Depending on intellectual qualities, one was then eligible for an assistant's job in the banquet or other service offices when an opening appeared. Many reached a certain level and stopped there. Mail clerks and concierges remained incumbent until they quit or died. A pleasant position along the way was that of telephone "chasseur" at one of the small switchboards on the Vendôme or Cambon side of the hotel. That was a desirable spot to be in, better than manning the elevators. If one listened but didn't repeat what he heard, there would be enough tips dropped in his palm to gladden his days.

The hotel's main telephone switchboard was "manned" by women. Females were also floor maids, laundresses, seamstresses and nurses.

A few bypassed the established formula. They were accountants, cashiers, sommeliers who knew the pedigrees and languages of wines, or those expert at mechanical, electrical and plumbing services. Talented bartenders could live out their lives mixing drinks, and several did. As Blanche would learn, they also supplied other valuable if illegal services.

Ten years after starting in the hotel, one might attain the supreme office, Managing Directeur.

"I have come in as manager," Claude reminded Blanche. "So, imagine what many must think of me—their consternation, waiting their turn."

She was proud of him for having been summoned to start so high, the first in the twenty-seven years of the hotel's existence. She discovered why the widow wanted him. Her son, Charles, had no ambition to take over, and she had found in Claude an experienced executive who was determined to emulate the precepts of César Ritz, and whose grasp of languages and courtesies would please her elegant clientele. He was also needed because her second-in-command, Victor Rey, was ailing.

Devoted to Rey, Marie Louise Ritz wanted to ease his work load. The tall, forbidding-looking woman lived with a personal maid, a pair of small furry dogs, and a flock of caged canaries. She could be seen at all hours, moving wraith-like through the hotel, seeking flaws in the operation and ways to achieve perfection, as her husband had tried to do. César Ritz is said to have slept at least once in every room in the hotel in order to test the mattresses.

Opposition to hiring Claude came from imperious Baron-Colonel Hans Pfyffer, but he was outvoted by Marie Louise and Victor Rey. The Baron-Colonel, who claimed both titles, had no set position within the hierarchy, but he was there and could make a lot of noise. He had inherited his place from his father, one of the hotel's original directors. The Pfyffers were Swiss, their titles derived from a long line of Pfyffers who had served as Vatican guards. The father, Colonel Hans Pfyffer d'Altishofen, architect and civil engineer, designed many hotels throughout Europe during the Second Empire. He took a liking to César Ritz when the boy was waiting on tables at the Hôtel de la Fidelité in Paris. The city, the hotel and the times were flush with wealth and beauty. Young César was entranced by the splendor around him, a stark contrast to what he had known at home, where he had herded cattle in summer and delivered firewood in winter.

The Hôtel de la Fidelité seemed the height of magnificence to the farm boy, but to Colonel Pfyffer it was spurious splendor. He had an affinity for plush and preached that money begets money. At his suggestion, César left the Fidelité for a similar job at the Hôtel Splendid in the Place de l'Opéra, mecca of millionaires. There, he ingratiated himself with J. Pierpont Morgan, John Wanamaker, Jay Gould, Commodore Vanderbilt and an assortment of Drakes, Drexels, Guggenheims and other affluent Americans.

Young Ritz studied their tastes and became convinced he could please them with a dream hotel. He reminisced later to Marie Louise Ritz, "In those years I had unheard-of courage

41

and worked with ardor, because I had plenty of ambition and little money."

He copied a coat of arms from a house in his native Niederwald, topped it with a royal crown that proclaimed Ritz, and was ready to stamp it on everything from the stationery to the silverware in his still imaginary hotel.

He was also a fop and an insufferable snob, but that combination, if not always likeable, made him a celebrated character on the great boulevards of Paris, London, Vienna, Madrid, Lisbon and Rome. His dream of a Paris Ritz was still ten years short of fulfillment when, in 1888, he married Marie Louise Beck. He was thirty-seven, had worked in all manner of capacities in various hotels of Europe, and knew exactly what he wanted, even in a wife. She had to be willing to work hard and to bear children, and she had to be young. Marie Louise, age twenty, filled all his requirements.

Charles, the first of their two sons, wasn't born until nine years later. By then César's cultivation of the rich and powerful had paid off. Millionaires, many risen from rough beginnings, were in awe of his regal manners, his insatiable search for perfection, and, incidentally, his immaculate dress.

He sported thirty business suits, forty-two fancy waistcoats, twelve sets of evening attire (but only eight silk hats), three hundred ties, and always appeared in public with a white carnation in his buttonhole. It made for an impressive entrance into the haunts of wealthy men, among whom were Calouste Gulbenkian, who dealt in oil and munitions and was rumored to be the richest man in the world; liquor manufacturer Marnier Lapostolle; and banker Edmond Rothschild. They helped Ritz finance the realization of his dream.

Learning this, Blanche asked Claude why, if Rothschild had helped back the hotel, there should be a policy against Jews.

"You must realize that among Jews there are also Jews who dislike Jews."

"See here," he told her, "that German woman who said the Ritz does not take Jews is mistaken. Every hotel has the right to turn away customers when they don't fit its image. Just last week, we refused a priest who came in drunk. It was done politely, of course. 'Sorry, we cannot find your request for a reservation. We regret that the hotel is full.' We would prefer actors and actresses go elsewhere, but we do take some. The same with Jews. There is a quota."

"So that's how I got in."

He looked pained. "Blanche, you are my wife. I would prefer we do not mention this subject again."

The subject was dropped, but it stayed in her mind. Later she said that that day materially affected her life.

"Being Jewish really wasn't important to me. I never ran into any restrictions back home on account of my religion, although I remember casting directors saying, 'You don't look Jewish.' Whether I did or didn't, it never mattered to me in New York. In Paris, I began to think about it. I loved being at the Ritz and wanted Claude to make a great success. The hotel was an incredible place—the men stood out, sharp, brilliant, the women were beautiful, and everybody was rich. It was audacious of me to think I could help Claude in such a place, but I had a feeling that I could."

5

"A woman without her man in bed with her is only half a woman."
—Claude Auzello

Adjustment to life in Paris was easy, bolstered, of course, by the splendor available to her at the Ritz.

Adjustment to matrimony wasn't easy. At first, it was money. He had a Frenchman's capacity for saving; she had an American's capacity for spending. Both were very good at it—talented, in fact.

It took more than a year to persuade him they should move. Finally, he gave in and granted permission. But it was illusory. Apartments in the first eight arrondissements, where she wanted to be, were impossible to find.

What he was saying was that if she could find one and it appealed to him, he would buy it. The nuance wasn't lost on her. And he said, "No agents! I will not pay an agent. They inflate prices."

He wanted to break her connection with Pearl White, who was becoming a red-blooded nuisance to the blue-bloods who saw her through lorgnettes and jaundiced eyes.

Pearl's assay into French films stopped after one; it somehow lacked the breathlessness of its American counterparts.

She signed for an engagement at the Casino de Paris but came up against a manic producer who devised an act in which she slid down a steep rope from the balcony, over the heads of the audience, to where a bull-like Apache dancer would grab her and throw her into flames billowing out of a trapdoor. There would be no net or other protective devices.

"The audience can follow me to the hospital where I'll take my bows," she said, and refused to do it. "Show me where the contract says I'm to kill myself on stage."

Instead she performed in a watered-down version, and soon

45

after opening night was subjected to a series of ominous and frightening phone calls. Police, obvious film fans, blamed them on Chinese and Germans. Nationals of both countries were always pictured as the villains who pursued her and failed in their missions. They suggested she leave France to save her life.

But business at the Casino was below expectations, the revue was a disaster, and Pearl told Blanche she was sure the producer was behind the threats. "I don't blame him," she added, and quit. Her cancellation was accepted with alacrity.

It was a brave show of independence.

Blanche said, "After she told me, I did something I haven't done in years. I got off by myself and sobbed and wept, and then I sobbed some more as though it was my heart and not hers that was breaking."

No one saw Pearl weep. She grew stout with fierce compulsions to overeat and over-drink.

Late one afternoon she created havoc when head bartender Frank Meier stopped her at the door to the Petit Bar, enforcing the "Men Only" edict. Unable to restrain Pearl's shouts or the homicidal way she swung her walking stick, he summoned Claude, who tried to explain the regulations to the star. Finally, it was necessary to hustle her into the street. A small truck that belonged to the hotel was at the service entrance, unloading foodstuffs. Blanche coaxed her into it, and they rode to Pearl's apartment singing bawdy songs.

Claude begged Blanche to end the friendship, but that sparked another argument that went unsettled. It was temporarily relieved when a new and handsome lover, Ted Cozzika, whisked Pearl out of Paris on a round-the-world trip.

As Victor Rey's illness grew in intensity, Claude's duties in the area of clientele relationship did likewise.

Marie Louise impressed on him that the desires of their guests, their every whim, fancy or complaint, had to have priority.

It struck Blanche that her husband was mainly required to help the female guests. "True," he told her. "Women take greater notice of irritations. It is a tribute to their instincts for perfection. In a hotel like the Ritz it is appreciated."

She was only partially mollified; but statistically she couldn't deny that females far outnumbered the males on the register.

The magnet that drew them was the survivors of a diminishing European aristocracy. Titles were immensely desirable in the wealthier bedrooms of America. Every ship from the States was depositing a bevy of debutantes at the reservation desk. Young ladies appeared to have sailed for France directly from their coming-out parties in quest of a regal-sounding mate.

Anna Gould had already solved that problem: she was the Duchess de Talleyrand-Périgord. She was searching for a permanent residence in Paris, and was prepared to spend a fortune for it. "Luckily I have more than one," she said. She occupied one of the hotel's most expensive suites.

She confided in Claude that she had a premonition she was going to be murdered in a hotel. Late one night he received a phone call that the Duchess had to see him. He dressed and went to her. She demanded he protect her.

"She is a formidable woman, and I needed formidable tact to have her continue as a guest in the hotel," he told Blanche. Keeping her tongue stuck conspicuously in her cheek, she agreed. It was a formidable feat, and he was to be congratulated.

The Duchess lost her fears and continued to pay a fat rent to the hotel until she found the mansion in the shadow of the Arc de Triomphe that suited her. Then, with the incredible wackiness that seemed commonplace among the abundantly endowed guests at the Ritz, she had the house she had long sought torn down and another, very different, built on the site. She stayed on during that period, too.

Blanche used the incident to gain something she dearly wanted. She suggested to Marie Louise that Claude could avoid delay in his late-night dealings with guests if *they* had a bed of their own in the hotel.

He was given a small set of rooms on the Cambon side to augment the flat in Passy. Blanche moved in her personal belongings, and, since no one connected with the hotel ever asked that she give up those rooms, she never did.

The opening lines in *Gentlemen Prefer Blondes*, the 1925 best seller by Anita Loos, set the locale at the Ritz. Ralph Barton's frontispiece depicts Lorelei Lee offering her dainty fingertips to a lecherous gent. Its caption: "Kissing your hand may make you feel very good but a diamond bracelet lasts forever."

The observant Miss Loos was a devotee of the hotel. Like her, Blanche was enthralled by its daily doings. And like Lorelei Lee, she was also fascinated by the evidence of wealth that permeated her surroundings at all hours.

The rooms that she and Claude now used on overnight occasions provided her with a close-up view of a ceremony performed each morning in the Vendôme lobby. Women guests appeared there with the gems they had worn the night before, spreading jewelry on tables to be checked by the concierge before being locked in the vault.

It was a dazzling show, worthy of palaces and museums. "You ought to charge admission," she told Claude. It was vulgar, too, but vulgarity didn't cross many minds in those elegant times. The acquisition of money and its usage for personal decoration seemed right and proper. It was how the privileged could show their love for their privileges. In no way—at least, at the Ritz—could it be considered a sign of social decadence. And in Blanche, those mornings stirred thoughts that would soon surface and vitally affect her life.

The mornings were exciting prologues to idyllic days, but Blanche's well-tuned antennae picked up one sour note. Amid the salutations of the personnel and the greetings from friendly guests, Hans Pfyffer looked the other way when she was near. Claude, who had noted that the Baron-Colonel was aloof to him, too, advised her to ignore the snub. Then the concierge on the Rue Cambon, knowing she was curious about everyone in range, whispered confidentially that Monsieur the Baron was anti-Semitic and knew she was a Jewess.

The concierge was a tactful observer of human nature.

Blanche admired the way he worked, with never a show of resentment, no matter how customer arrogance erupted. He hid his true feelings under layers of submission, cooperation, smiles, tolerance, civility, bows and charm. "That is how he must be," Claude told her. "If it were in my province, I would fire any worker who argues with a guest."

She suspected that she knew more than he did about the workers whose tolerances went beyond simple obeisance. Ask for an abortionist, a smuggler, a forger, perhaps a killer— nothing phased the tolerant workers of the Ritz in their efforts to please.

Her discoveries that all things were possible at the Ritz made it easy to take a step that she hoped would improve Claude's future. She couldn't do much about Pfyffer and his prejudices, but she could take steps to offset others.

She decided to change her religion. She simply needed a little help from a free-wheeling hireling and the unwitting cooperation of the United States government.

Frank Meier, the all-purpose bartender, never betrayed a confidence. He summoned a young wizened Levantine, who went by the pseudonym of Greep, for a rendezvous with Blanche. There was nothing furtive about it; they met in the sunshine at a table at the Café de la Paix, and he undertook to handle her problem for one hundred American dollars and the small cost of his chain-drinking coffee habit. He never touched liquor, he said, pointing a finger to his eye and saying, "See! I am a smart fellow."

He ranked, he told her, with the foremost artists in his profession. He would take care of every detail littering the pages in her passport that required official scrutiny. Instead of listing her parents as Sara and Isaac Rubenstein, her birthplace as New York, and her religion as Jewish, her passport would identify her as Blanche Ross, a name derived from her movie career, her parents as Jane and George Ross, her birthplace as Cleveland, Ohio, and her religion as Catholic.

"While you're at it, can you knock two years off my age?"

He nodded, looking carefully at her face. "Nobody will question."

"In that case," she said, "knock off four."

He came back in a few days, his work done.

"You know this place, Cleveland?"

"It's in the Middle West," she said.

He screwed up his already well-creased face and advised her to memorize as many features of that city as she could. "Today it is not of much importance, but who knows what will happen tomorrow."

She would remember, ruefully, how she neglected his suggestion; but when she did, it was a very different decade.

As he boasted, he did his work well. She presented the fraudulent document, which needed an early renewal, to the embassy. The passport division, indifferent to genealogical truth, soon produced a new and official copy which now included her married name, too. She proudly showed Claude that she was now Blanche Ross Auzello, with an entirely fictitious background and entry into the world.

He was appalled.

"I do not understand how you are without feeling for your religious heritage!"

"Idiot! Perhaps I love you more!"

Later he said, "If we have a child, we shall have to tell the truth. It would not be fair, otherwise."

Whether or not to have a child had been the subject of many pillow talks. Children were subdued rarities in the hotel. Those seen had to be well bred or restrained by parents and nannies. If they weren't, they were politely admonished by the management. The Ritz preferred children already grown.

A conclave of doctors had just given the world their theory that modern women could bear children at forty-five. That seemed a tacit permission. It made the waiting okay. As a side comfort for Claude, the doctors agreed that a man could function forever and father a child at eighty (if he had the energy for it). "It will require no more than it takes to lift a six-story building," stated one sardonic French newspaperman.

50

They decided to wait—not too long, perhaps three years, five at the outside. "For love of the Ritz," said Blanche.

Celebrating their anniversary, Victor Rey provided a party on the terrace and offered a champagne toast: "Our Auzello is a doubly happy man, for he has two great loves: his wife and the hotel!"

It was repeated many times to anyone who asked about the new manager, as if engraved on his identification card. Then, at breakfast one morning, soon after he told Blanche he loved her almost beyond human endurance, he veered into what seemed to her an irrelevant lecture on the imbalance between the male and female populations of France. "We are a civilized country. . . . Naturally, we cannot drown girl babies as savages do. No . . . it is a pitiful thing, really, that many women in France are forced into loneliness and frustrations while we kill men with wars. We have had a hundred years of wars. The men of France are decimated; they engage in a mass suicide pact. I know, I have seen it."

"That's very interesting, Claude. I never thought of that."

"That's why I say to you, a woman without her man in bed with her is only half a woman."

"Oh?"

"So, you see why it is necessary that I have this other woman? Yes, I shall no longer sleep at home on Thursdays."

Her spirited refusal to permit any such arrangement erupted into the usual accoutrements of domestic strife: her objections, his insistences, shouts and finally a door slammed violently from the outside.

It wasn't going to be easy to leave Paris.

While she packed, she thought, "I am a sophisticated woman; I ought to laugh at this. But I can't."

It wasn't going to be easy to pick up life in New York again.

Growing up there had been exciting, years of fun and anticipation. Anticipation that wore thin, that promised wonders that didn't materialize; disappointments that blotted out the happier times like an impenetrable asbestos curtain coming down.

51

Looking back, suddenly, after Claude stormed out, she could only see the annoyances. Driving home from Observation Point with sullen, beaver-coated adolescents who felt that necking was a jumping-off point for busy hands and lustful tongues. Winter mornings in a thin evening gown, riding the ferries to Fort Lee, shivering all the way. Heading into her thirties with revised views about the acting ability she would need to be a film star.

Paris was the pick-me-up one needed for a New York hangover. It removed the headache, restored the appetite. It was colorful and comfortable. It was where gorgeous little shops locked arms with inviting sidewalk cafés. Where one could enjoy her mornings with nothing more on her mind than what to wear to a fashion show or a luncheon. She was living in indolence and loving it. It would take fortitude to run away from it.

Claude had all the freedom he wanted to devote to the job he loved. He was occupied with it day and night. But, she thought, if he is so damn busy every minute, he can only enjoy a mistress on my time. Jealousy swept away all contemplation of her new, beautiful life. That other woman had to be someone he wanted to be with, and he was probably in bed with her that very moment. His phrase "Always, Parisians love love the best" rang in her mind.

The more furiously that image rose in her, the more resolute she became. She would share her husband with the Ritz, but not with another woman. If he wanted another female he could have her, but he couldn't have his wife too.

Having reacted conventionally, she would go all the way, do the conventional thing, go home to mother. Claude was not a generous man, but she had enough money on hand to get to New York. She would start for it at once, but not in one fast leap. Ocean liners sailed the Atlantic on schedules that required advance bookings. However, she could cross the English Channel without delay and let her absence reveal to him the extent of her anger.

She packed a steamer trunk, two suitcases and two hat boxes and caught the night train to London.

"I was mad as hell," she said. "Not only at his wanting another woman, but the way he broke the news. Imagine trying to justify a mistress for patriotic reasons!"

Claude rationalized his actions this way: "Ninety-nine out of a hundred times one goes about it without a word to his wife. I told her because I loved her. I thought she would understand, but she showed no appreciation at all!"

A bumpy roadbed and her tossing berth while the sleeping car was shunted around and ferried from Calais to Dover kept her awake through a long night. Those sleepless hours only strengthened her resolve not to concede. There could be no compromise, no half-reconciliations; that was her position. It was all or nothing.

"I never tried to influence men with tears," she reflected many years later. "It was not my style. I just got the hell out and was damned if I would let him know where to find me."

But that part of her resolve was short-lived.

At Victoria Station, faced by porters asking her destination, she remembered that London had a Ritz, too. Built by the backers of César Ritz, it was licensed to carry his name and operated in harmony with its Paris counterpart. It was a fast shift of strategy, a slight bending of resolve, but she decided it wouldn't hurt her cause if she provided Claude with a hint where to contact her.

She checked in as Mrs. Claude Auzello, and a personal call from the manager to welcome her made it seem likely he would relay word of her presence to Paris. But her phone remained quiescent, as if in tune with the hushed atmosphere of the somber hotel and the grey city, both as reserved as the nature of England itself and as austere as any of its cathedrals.

Just in case, she put off booking a departure for New York.

She wandered through the West End streets, pleased to hear English spoken all around her again. But the weather was wet and the people dry and preoccupied, in solemn comparison to the ways of Paris. Lonely meanderings through Selfridge's and long tea breaks at Fortnum and Mason's raised doubts in her mind whether she really should have retreated from the marital battleground.

53

"What's more," she reflected later, "I hated English food. God knows they had the ingredients; they just didn't know what to do with them."

Two days later, with no word from Claude, she was very dispirited. Even the theaters, acknowledged as the best in the world, held no attraction for her, though the season was highlighted by Americans—Pauline Lord in Eugene O'Neill's *Anna Christie* and George M. Cohan in *So This Is London*. The mail clerk at the hotel's front desk, having no messages to offer, assured her its agencies could help her buy tickets to the city's smash hits. But she vetoed the idea. If Claude called at night, she wanted to be there.

He didn't call.

Placards of newspaper hawkers on the street corners blazed with huge pronouncements: SHOCK AT OLD BAILEY and PRINCESS TRIAL SENSATION. Amazed, Blanche discovered that Marguerite Laurent, the French woman she had met the afternoon she attended the races with J'Ali, was accused of murdering her husband, Prince Fahmi-Bey.

A taxi took her to the turreted Old Bailey, where the trial was underway. But sightseers overflowed and further admission was closed. She was losing a lively argument with the sergeant at arms when a group of men emerged, and amongst them, a most familiar figure. She called, "J'Ali!" And in an instant he had her in an impassioned embrace.

They lunched at an Islamic restaurant in Soho, where she fabricated her reason for being in London. It was a shopping tour, she lied, because Claude's new affluence since moving to the Ritz made it necessary they relocate in a fine apartment in Paris and she planned to decorate it with the best antiques London could provide.

He was on a very different mission, and his voice and emotions rose as he explained he was there to see that justice was meted out to Marguerite, who had shot and killed his best friend after six months of marriage.

"She will die screaming," he raged. Then, "But never mind, my angel. It is a gift of Allah, finding you here."

However, she would not agree to the reunion he wished to

have. Thoroughly disturbed by Claude's silence, she spent another evening alone in her room, then gladly accepted J'Ali's invitation to accompany him to the third session of the trial.

The Fahmi-Bey marriage had terminated in a burst of gunfire in a bedroom in the Savoy Hotel. According to defense testimony, a few months had changed a gay, fascinating bride into a wretched, broken wife. Then, on a stormy night of violent lightning and thunder, which appeared to her counsel as symbolic of the soul of the tormented Marguerite, she shot Fahmi three times with his Browning automatic, which, it was alleged, went off when she was actually trying to unload it. Each time she pulled back the mechanism to remove a cartridge, it was indeed removed, but through the barrel and right into her husband's guts.

The defense was in the hands of Edward Marshall Hall, a giant among British barristers. A prominent French woman *avocat* was expected to defend her, but Marguerite wanted Hall, a compelling figure in his long white wig and floor-length black robe, his high white collar above and silver-buckled shoes below. He was an audacious actor of superb intensity, and the spectators, with the exception of the Egyptians amongst them, were stunned with admiration by the theatrics he presented as he fought for his client's life. The defendant watched him with such admiration that few could doubt that her preference for him was from the heart. It took only a few moments for Blanche to see that.

She and J'Ali favored opposite sides. She reacted angrily as the leading prosecutor for the Crown promised that Marguerite, an alien on British soil, would not escape justice. Addressing the jury, he said, "Coming to this country, persons are bound by the laws which prevail here, just as we, who are native-born. From her own lips it is known that it was she who caused the death of her husband. And, in the absence of any circumstances to make it some other offense, you must find her guilty of murder."

Powerful and resentful Egyptians, including J'Ali, sitting beside Blanche, shouted approval. They had brought in lawyers of their own, hoping to buttress the prosecution. But Marshall Hall lashed out violently at the character of the dead man and the nature of the land he came from. He called Fahmi a world-weary pleasure-seeker with vicious and eccentric sexual appetites.

Probing the cause for the shooting, he attributed his client's motivation for taking her husband's life to "unbelievable practices." It was a dramatic moment in the court. The prosecution's declaration that "accidental firing of a gun" wasn't sufficient excuse made Hall decide to drop his planned line of defense and gamble on a new, desperate attack.

Fahmi-Bey manhandled her and forced her into incredible perverted actions, he maintained, causing her to dread night, loathing what she knew he meant to do to her.

"I have suffered terribly," testified the defendant through a translator, as counsel guided her through the labyrinth of her marriage. "Once," she said, "Fahmi-Bey picked up a book, kissed it and said, 'I swear on the Koran that I will kill you and you shall die by my hand.'" After which she added, somewhat naïvely, "I began to understand he was not very sincere in his love for me."

It was brought out that she had refused to change her religion to that of her husband and, as a consequence, Fahmi-Bey drew up a one-sided marriage contract. She was forbidden the right to divorce him, but he could dissolve their marriage at will.

Blanche was fascinated, of course, for J'Ali often spoke of the Koran, the sacred writing of Allah. He had once told her, too, that any legal union within his circle would have to be based upon a contract that he contrived.

Blanche's already charged emotions were further fired up as she heard details of the climax of Marguerite's disastrous relationship. The coincidence wasn't lost on her; she had moved to the brink of such a close liaison with J'Ali that he, too, might have subjected her to obedience in bed that satisfied his id and his ego. Suddenly—and despite all her earlier resolutions—she was overwhelmed with a desire to speak to Claude, to ascertain how he was faring without her and to let him know she missed him.

She left the court and telephoned Claude in Paris. He had to be paged before he took the call. Finally his voice came through. "Look here," he said brusquely, "you have come to your senses?"

She admitted that she missed him, whereupon he waited a long time and then said, "Come back, Blanchette, and we will work out these problems." When she hesitated, he added humbly, "There is a void in my life without you."

But the climactic moment was on hand in court, and she wanted to be there for it. Claude knew about the case; Marguerite was getting heroine treatment in the French press.

"I feel terribly sorry for her," Blanche said. "I want to be here if she needs me."

Forthright as usual, she told him J'Ali had made arrangements for her to attend.

"Ah! He has turned up again, eh?"

She explained it was an accidental meeting. "I did not leave Paris for him. You know that. Tell me I can stay. Trust me."

"See here, I will trust you, but not this Prince."

She laughed. "Darling, I will be on tomorrow night's train to Paris, no matter what happens in court."

In Marshall Hall's address on the fourth day of the trial, he said, "I daresay the Egyptian civilization is, and may be, one of the oldest and most wonderful civilizations in the world. The curse of this case is the atmosphere we in the West cannot understand, the perversions of the Turk in his harem, the possession of women. . . . Just imagine its effect on this poor girl, outraged, abused, beaten, degraded . . ."

To illustrate the shooting, he imitated the crouch of the stealthy, advancing Fahmi, moving dramatically between two rows of chairs, a performance that watching reporters wrote "made his hearers' flesh creep."

In a tour-de-force performance, Hall changed from the predatory Fahmi to the horror-stricken Marguerite, holding the murder weapon, and then, in the hush of a mesmerized courtroom, he snapped the trigger three times and dropped the gun onto the tile floor of the Old Bailey. It was a spectacular climax; all those in the room literally jumped out of their seats.

"Members of the jury," he pleaded, "open the gates that this Western woman can go out, not into the dark night of the desert, but into the light of God's great Western sun!" Then he pointed up at the skylight, and the packed and spellbound court looked at the rays streaming in and suffusing the defendant in warmth and brightness. It was a supremely effective finish. In one hour, the jury returned a verdict of acquittal.

The cheers from the spectators, in which Blanche joined, were so voluminous that the judge ordered the courtroom cleared. Ignoring J'Ali's anger, Blanche fought the tide of spectators and gained Marguerite's attention by shouting felicitations in French. When the overjoyed woman recognized her, Blanche wrote on a card, "I am no longer at the Claridge; I am Madame Auzello at the Ritz. Call me."

J'Ali was waiting outside. "I have the claim on you. Not that woman." He pulled the locket he had sworn to wear from inside his shirt. "Here. I have been faithful. We must go away together."

She held out her hand. "Au revoir."

He folded his arms and said, "We are not yet finished, my angel."

She signaled a cab and left him there.

Reporting on the trial, the BBC announced that the President of the Barristers of Egypt had cabled the Attorney-General of Great Britain, complaining that Marshall Hall had allowed himself to generalize in lashing out at Egypt, and, indeed, the whole of the East. "A great advocate like Hall is not ignorant," the cable stated, "that it is unjust and disloyal to judge a whole nation by the conduct of a single individual."

It was all in the Paris papers that she knew Claude would see. "Personally," she said, "I wasn't going to judge J'Ali by the bedroom antics of Prince Fahmi-Bey."

On departing London, she was escorted to her train by minions of the Ritz. "Precisely," the porter told her, as they did all titled Britishers who were leaving, with red carpet and high officials of the railway on hand "to see to the comforts."

She headed for Paris apprehensively, but Claude was waiting on the platform when she stepped onto it.

It was a memorable moment for them. Both were caught in a flood of sentiment for the other, but in their own way. She gave him a passionate kiss, and he held her in a compassionate embrace.

He said, "You have learned how much you need me, eh?"

She said, "You bastard, it's the other way around." She gave him a playful slap on the cheek, and he gave her one on the derriere. Then he held her in a long kiss while the porter holding her bags waited resignedly. Then they followed him into the great, crowded, noisy Gare du Nord, arm in arm.

"We will go straight to bed," he told her, "and never speak of the nights we have been apart."

He thought she had accepted his right to a mistress; she thought he had given up the idea.

Both were wrong.

6

"Fashion without style is meaningless."
—Coco Chanel

Early in autumn of 1927, Blanche made a triumphal reappearance in New York, a reconciliation present from Claude, who arranged for her to spend ten days at the Ritz-Carlton Hotel.

Her family didn't frequent the Ritz-Carlton often; it was one of the most stylish hotels in the city. She didn't tell them that her Popsy got a special rate. She wanted to build up his image, make him seem more important than he was. She showed snapshots to prove he was handsome and sexy, and used stories to tell of his intimacies with the world-famous and to evidence his generosity. She displayed a diamond brooch and emerald pin and let them believe they were gifts from Claude—although they'd been given to her by J'Ali, and Claude wouldn't let her wear them in Paris.

"Every American woman puts on airs in Paris," she said. "I did the same thing in New York."

She had stories about her own encounters with celebrities. She had asked Gertrude Stein, the stocky grey-haired writer who wore her hair pompadour-style, if her name was actually Rubenstein. "You look like my father," she explained. According to her, she meant it as a compliment, but there is no record that Gertrude Stein accepted it as one.

There were no get-togethers with brother Herman, who had joined the musicians' safari to Hollywood the year before, when sound had invaded the movies. He had stature as a lyricist at last, writing theme songs without which no movie of the day seemed complete. Over the long-distance phone, he and Blanche exchanged regrets at their separation, and voiced pride in each other's accomplishments. He told her he loved her more than anyone else on earth, which was probably true, and also said he had licked the drug habit, which was not.

Claude traveled to Cherbourg to be at the ship when she returned. A long day of travel there and back, a long day away from the hotel. On the train to Paris they talked about the hotel as if it were their child; as most people do when they haven't seen each other for a while, they discussed the ups and downs of the family while they were apart.

Victor Rey was feeling better; Colonel Pfyffer was healthier than ever and getting closer to Marie Louise Ritz; a young telephone chasseur, Georges Scheuer, who had been promoted to the Cambon Bar, was doing well and was next in line to take over from Frank Meier.

With his love for anecdotes, Claude had a fund of stories about the hotel personnel, past and present, which filled the time as their train roared toward Paris—about the great *chefs de cuisine* Escoffier, Olivier, Gimon and . . . But Blanche wanted to know about him. How was he getting along?

He was enthusiastic about his duties, busier than ever. There were new types of guests, made wealthy by the surge of prosperity that was filling everyone's pockets with gold, ten years after the Kaiser's War. But instead of talking about himself, he was off on stories about others. For instance, the rich Greeks . . .

Niarchos, one of the wealthiest, gave a luncheon for twenty guests. But he sat by himself at a neighboring table, thinking, making notes, never speaking to the others. When the meal ended, he picked up the full check and they all left. Peculiar, those Greeks.

Blanche pressed for more about himself. "Peculiar, you French," she said. "You keep talking about everything but what I want to hear. Isn't it time for you to be promoted?"

He shook his head, smiling indulgently. "See here, there is no further promotion possible. Victor Rey is the Managing Directeur. I told you, he is feeling better. Would you want to see him die so I win a promotion?"

She didn't answer him directly. Just a slight shrug. An impish look that implied it wasn't a bad idea.

"Peculiar, you Americans," he said. She couldn't disagree.

"I wasn't as happy in New York as I expected to be. Anyway, I'm glad to be back."

He was glad she was back, too, but not everyone would be. He didn't tell her that in her absence Baron Pfyffer had complained that she was too brash, that given the chance she would try to run the hotel her way, usurping the position of the woman who had the right to it.

"Your wife wishes to be queen here," he told Claude. "It is Marie Louise's position. I should like you to know I have warned Marie Louise of this."

If he meant to upset Claude, he succeeded. Although Marie Louise continued to be cordial, he was sure the Baron must have upset her, too. Within the incestuous closeness of the hotel family, the power struggle never ceased.

She was impatient to get back. The very sight of the huge carriage-type lamps jutting out from the hotel's doorways was like beacons drawing a homesick sailor into harbor.

The Ritz was her Utopia. Its lobbies, corridors, *galeries*, rooms, suites, bars, salons, restaurants, gardens and terraces, pavilions and promenades were the galaxies making up her cosmos. It was a walled-in universe.

She had become an habituée. Attendance was an addiction. All *reguliers* greeted each other with kisses and handshakes. They couldn't let a day pass without an appearance. If anyone did miss a day, all acted as if they had been apart for weeks.

The terrace tables filled early. Blanche had learned to recognize the social climbers moving up and down on the social seesaw. She believed she could keep her balance and see through the hypocrisy, narcissism, exhibitionism and flattery. But if she didn't mingle, she would miss the gossip of the day, gossip of Paris, London, New York. It was worth risking contagion for that.

The gossip came in all languages. She could speak French

by this time. Claude saw to it, giving her lessons until, finally, he said, "Enough. I cannot improve your pronunciation, and if I continue, you will ruin mine."

Social arbiter E. Berry Wall always made his appearance at four o'clock, and Frank Meier had his usual large brandy snifter of hot champagne ready for him. When Wall praised Blanche's use of the native tongue, Claude smiled affectionately and said, "Ah, yes, she speaks approximate French."

In the late afternoon, when the breeze seeped through and the terrace turned cool, the *reguliers* moved to their favorite watering places on the Cambon side. Their established habits inspired J. Ainsworth Morgan of Santa Barbara, idling in Europe after Princeton and Oxford, to compose an *Ode to the Ritz Bar* that began this way:

> *Good morning mister, sir or count,*
> *What will it be today?*
> *And Frank awaits the deft reply:*
> *"The same as yesterday."*

For the men it was just a step inside from the street entrance. The hotel called it the Petit Bar, the French called it the Cambon Bar, and the Americans called it the Ritz Bar.

In it, elderly Europeans tried to isolate themselves as best they could from the convivial overseas drinkers who crowded uncomfortably against them.

The Americans wore loud clothes and had voices to match and displayed manic intensity in their drinking and dice-throwing contests.

Backgammon was a hot betting game. The men were oblivious to the room across the vestibule that they called the Chatterbox, where their ladies-in-waiting loitered, in their own fashion, in a mix of *La Bohème* and *La Vie Parisienne*, munching hors d'oeuvres and pastries or feeding them to their well-coiffed Pekinese and poodles. Dogs of both sexes were permitted everywhere in the hotel; only humans were segregated.

The decor fitted feminine tastes. It was no accident; it was planned that way. In the early days of the electric light, when bulbs were prominent attention-getters, César Ritz found their whiteness too glaring. He sat his wife under varied colored bulbs while he tried them on her complexion, her jewelry and her clothes. He settled on a delicate apricot-pink and made it the theme of the hotel's lamps. In his innovative way, he also pioneered indirect lighting, for he used alabaster urns to throw gleams from the bulbs up onto the ceiling instead of down onto the floor.

From the men's point of view, the women appeared engaged in ladylike pastimes, but they were actually reveling in very personal secrets about their partners, visible across the way.

They threw conversational spotlights on the men in their lives as if each were a performer doing a specialty onstage. Their lovers were undressed and stripped naked by their tongues, their physical parts described, their abilities catalogued, bed habits and styles of fornication revealed. This, according to Blanche, was how the ladies of the Chatterbox took revenge for being fenced off.

Claude surprised Blanche with how much he knew about what went on. She accused him of planting a spy, which he denied. She decided, then, that it was logical for him to know, for in emulating César Ritz he sought to learn everything about everywhere in the hotel. She figured he got secret reports from the sharp-eared serving maids who were in and out at all hours.

Among zanies making the Ritz a hangout, Harry Crosby was a standout. An ineffectual poet, he could afford to chase the muse with financial help from his American family, but not to the point that it interfered with his drinking.

On the occasion of the annual Beaux-Arts Ball, he brought pandemonium to the hotel by leading in a motley mob of half-naked students, mostly boys but some girls, who spread out, beating tom-toms, throwing confetti everywhere, creating hell and chaos, and finally retreated before Claude, who was not amused, and a few underlings, who were.

A few hours later, having taken the group to Les Halles for

the traditional early-morning onion soup, Crosby returned to the hotel on a loaded vegetable cart. A few days after that, having organized a four-carriage race from the Etoile to the Cambon Bar, he came whooping through the portals, the winner. His black whippet, Narcisse Noir, wearing a gold mesh collar that resembled a necklace, stepped daintily beside him.

All Harry Crosby types, and Paris had many, sent shudders of disapproval through Claude.

"We have become less of a hotel and more of a circus." He felt it was due to indifference from Baron Pfyffer, the aloofness of Marie Louise, and inadequate controls by Victor Rey, again in uncertain health.

His frustration over his own impotent position propelled him into morose moods, and that affected Blanche. The young enthusiast she had married was behaving as if he were ten years older than his age. At least ten. She didn't want that to happen to her.

"There comes a time in everyone's life when they wonder what would have happened if they had chosen differently."

London was not the end of J'Ali. He sent flowery notes to her at the Ritz, letters from Egypt and Turkey and then New York and Texas. The mail desk passed them on, along with a flow of mail from acquaintances keeping a line open in case they needed reservations in the hotel. The general quantity of mail swelled in the spring, but J'Ali's messages were constant and seemingly sincere.

"I never figured out what held me back in London; J'Ali was more attractive than ever, he wanted me, and I should have let myself go. What with Popsy's devotion to the hotel and his probable involvement with another woman, I began to kick myself. I thought that if I saw J'Ali again . . ."

He was also in her mind because Marguerite Fahmi-Bey, now known familiarly to Blanche as Maggy, was back in Paris.

Since her trial, she had acquired the estate of her slain husband and lost a great deal of her naïveté. She said it would be no problem for Claude to discover what went on in the all-female room. She was sure that every one of the serving maids was his mistress.

Only one would reign as favorite, she thought, but that was Blanche's problem. "Today one, tomorrow another."

The Princess had purchased a princely apartment at 22, Place Vendôme, directly across the square. Addicted to stylish and showy hats and expensive furs, she made the Ritz her parlor. She enjoyed great wealth and great cynicism.

She was sure of Claude's extra-sexual activities because of an involvement of her own with a married man, the barrister who had won her her freedom. "He's the smartest there is, and he says no man has the ability to be faithful."

Marshall Hall journeyed into Paris and Maggy's arms as often as possible. Blanche was the go-between. Cables foretold his coming. Requests for rooms at the Ritz were signals Blanche conveyed. Discreetly.

Few who saw or mingled with her in the hotel had any idea that Maggy Fahmi-Bey was once publicly called a murderess. But she was a picturesque fixture that could not be ignored. The curious invariably asked, "Who's the lady with the hat?" In response to those inquiries, the hotel staff volunteered that she was very rich and lived across the street. Claude saw to it that no more than that was said. He was a determined foe of notoriety.

But doubts whether he had a mistress were dispelled when he announced that henceforth he would be away on Thursday nights.

"See here," he said, "I have found a woman who is sweet, genteel, very discreet. She is French. She will never make trouble for you."

"Is she someone I know?"

He shook his head.

"But she knows me?"

"She has seen you. Yes."

"So I've seen her."

He shrugged. "That does not matter."

"It does to me. You obviously prefer her to me."

"See here, that's preposterous. Of course I do not."

She stared at him.

He said, "I cannot make you understand."

"On that, at least, we agree."

But thereafter, on Thursdays, she slept alone.

He suggested to Marie Louise Ritz that the time had come to admit women into the bar with the men. Blanche took it as part of his conciliatory moves toward her. He knew she wanted the barriers removed, even though he still preferred all the old César Ritz traditions. Just making the suggestion had to be a measure forced by love rather than preference.

However, whether by decision of Marie Louise or of Baron Pfyffer, the ladies and gentlemen stayed put.

Among the segregated females, Blanche began looking at every one as her Thursday-night rival. Describing her as French didn't make it so. "My God, Blanche. Don't look at me," said Maggy Fahmi-Bey.

Blanche assured her she was above suspicion. "I bit my tongue to keep from saying she could not be the one because Popsy didn't like her."

But none was entirely excluded. She kept on looking and continued to shake hands and bestow kisses on all her acquaintances every day, carefully on the watch for telltale clues.

There were the Dolly Sisters, Rosie and Jenny. They were momentarily single, having shed their American song-writing husbands. Both were demon gamblers, devoted attendees at the baccarat clubs. Their losses were enormous; Claude could neither afford nor tolerate such a lifestyle.

"All men lie," according to Maggy. "Not Claude," said Blanche. According to what he said, his mistress was sweet, genteel and discreet. There were a few strangers every day, and on them she concentrated much of her attention. Did she smoke too much (he wouldn't like that), drink too much (ditto), laugh too loud, or was she overdressed, overweight or overage? She could eliminate any woman on those counts. ("I always gave Claude credit for good taste.")

Therefore she could eliminate the sexy lady with the 250-

carat "stomacher" just purchased at Cartier. Claude admitted he loved large bosoms, but that woman's equipment was over-powering. But there was in the hotel a very quiet, aloof woman who often smiled at Blanche but never spoke, who signed all her checks but never tipped. Perhaps Claude was supporting her.

But she was not the one. From Claude, Blanche learned she was a princess being discarded by a husband with royal con-nections in the Balkans. Victor Rey had extended unlimited credit for her food and rent, but word had come to the hotel that a divorce settlement was blocked and the state would not honor her bill. ("See here, it is a difficult situation. Even un-limited credit has limits, you know.")

Then the woman managed, with the sale of a bracelet, to settle her accounts, and she moved out.

So the search went on.

The leading celebrity in the Chatterbox was Mrs. Jack Dean, professionally known as Mrs. Fanny Ward. She held court while her husband played backgammon across the corridor for excessively high stakes.

Her Broadway stage triumphs were formidable, but she was most celebrated for her well-publicized battles against fading youth. A pretty, petite woman, her skin drawn tight across her whitely powdered face, she was panicked by middle age. She was not alone in that; nobody at the Ritz was middle-aged. It was as if there were no such thing: you were young or you were old.

A female Ponce de Leon, she left Paris at times for treat-ments from Dr. Serge Voronoff in Switzerland, whose monkey-gland treatments, he claimed, would stay the onrush of time. She returned with her hair a little blonder, her cheeks less wrinkled, but her voice more gravelly and her age a guarded secret.

Knowing Blanche was still seeking the identity of Claude's mistress while he was equally determined to prevent it, Mrs. Ward volunteered two words of sage advice:

"Forget it."

Discovery, she warned, would stir a *contretemps* that would end badly for her. She had seen wives destroy the love they were trying to save.

"The mistress won't ruin the marriage, but quite often the wife will."

However, Claude's Thursday-night absences were very hard to take. Each new pretty face was inspected. Could she be the one?

At last Blanche was sure who she was. The woman drinking tea each afternoon was doll-like and demure, and, as their acquaintanceship progressed, admitted to an amorous affair while zealously protecting the name of her lover.

"There are complications," she explained. Her smile was charming, but women, Blanche always contended, could be perfidious, and perhaps Michelle, her new friend, was playing a game of cat and mouse, as it were, with Blanche the mouse. Actually hating herself for it, she decided to follow her.

"I knew I was being a damn fool, but I could be as stubborn as Claude when I wanted to be."

On a Thursday night she hid in a doorway across from Michelle's *pied à terre* in the Rue de Lille, suspended between a terrible anxiety and the fear that Claude would appear.

It was a hot autumn night, the windows open everywhere, light curtains failing to hide rooms or occupants.

Finally Michelle's lover arrived, a tall, powerfully built woman. The tightness of their embrace, before they drew the blinds, left little doubt as to the relationship.

Blanche tiptoed away, reached a bench on the quai near the Pont Royal, and sat, shaking with laughter.

"The idiocy of what I was doing struck me. I wanted to scream, it was so funny."

A pair of lovers sat down alongside her, saw the odd look on her face, asked if she was sick.

"I was," she told them. "But I have just been cured."

Early in December 1929, an avalanche of cancellations descended on the hotel in the wake of the Wall Street crash. Cables poured in from America amidst telephone calls from

Le Havre and Cherbourg. All brought the same bad news. Trips were being postponed; customers who had heard of their ruination aboard ocean liners were going back without coming ashore.

It was related in the bar—probably apocryphally—that one thoughtful fellow left a note for the purser of the *Olympic* to cancel his suite at the Ritz just before he leaped off the deck and drowned.

Fashion-show buyers, who customarily fluttered about like robins in the spring, canceled their reservations before Christmas.

When spring arrived, its usual fresh beauty pervaded the trees, parks, *rues* and boulevards of Paris, but in the hotel, signs of disaster were all too plain. For the first time in its history, empty beds outnumbered those occupied.

The hotel was suffering from realities unknown since Claude had begun his duties; concierges pretended to be busy, doormen waited at portals that didn't need to be opened, bellboys listened for bells that didn't ring, barmen wiped glasses already glistening with polish, waiters stood morosely by unoccupied tables, phones were quiet. The emptiness was painful. There were wholesale cuts in personnel.

Personally responsive to those conditions, Claude experienced a psychogenic interaction. He, too, was desolate.

He sliced Blanche's already spare allowance and tightened the strings around her household expenditures. Ironically, long-sought apartments became available just when he couldn't afford to move. And J'Ali didn't help matters with a note saying he had won enough at Monte Carlo to add to his holdings—now he had a villa on the sea, near Alexandria.

She decided that in some ungiven time she would go to Egypt. In the gloom pervading the empty rooms on the Place Vendôme, it was an exhilarating thought.

7

"Claude acted as though Wall Street crashed right on top of him," observed Blanche.

Empty and morose, like the hotel, he filled his slack hours reading history. He was exasperated by her disinterest in the subject.

After work, he led her straight to the Métro and home to Passy. She tried to detour toward theaters showing the new talking films, but then he became the disinterested one. He would drop into his favorite chair while she resigned herself to solitaire. "I'm going to be a hundred before I'm thirty-five," she told him.

"Must you live in tension? Can't you read a book?"

"I've read a book."

He didn't think it funny, but she did. "One of my chums at Lindy's said that once."

"Study history, Blanchette. It leads from the past to the future."

"Lindy's is part of my past."

He urged her to read up on Napoleon.

"France needs another like him, I can tell you. But where is he?"

"You're asking me?"

He found a book for her and held it out. "Here. Begin the study of history with Napoleon."

She exploded. "Oh, Popsy! To hell with history!"

He threw down the book and went to bed.

From history it was a short step to present-day politics, but she had no interest in that either.

Adolf Hitler, whom she characterized as a clown with Charlie's mustache but not his talent, was beginning to dominate all central European leaders. Claude called him a mountebank and rabble-rouser and was incensed when he denounced France as the implacable enemy of the German people. Allies and opponents were forming teams; battle lines were being drawn.

Claude, however, was confident that France had finally learned one lesson of history and could stop such manic politicians. Perhaps Minister of War André Maginot would be the successor to Napoleon. He had begun his military career as a sergeant, a notch above the immortal corporal. A good sign.

He had authorized construction of an impregnable shield, something new in warfare, a fortified trench to stretch from border to border. Claude wholeheartedly approved the notion.

"The one flaw I have perceived in Bonaparte's tactics is that he fought every battle the same. Wellington perceived it too. Otherwise we French would have won the contest at Waterloo." In Claude's phraseology, Napoleon's antagonists always contested him, never defeated him.

"You think there'll be another war?"

Her question pleased him. "Aha! I have interested you at last!" He had a ready answer. "For France, there is always another war!"

"Will you have to go?"

"Naturally. Whenever war comes I shall fight. But first I will send you back to America."

Slowly, the Ritz recovered.

Its guest list grew healthy again, but not in quite the same way. Many who dribbled in were Americans on a first trip to Paris.

They discovered Blanche and invited her on their shopping tours, to translate and check prices and find bargains and save money. For introducing these spenders of dollars, merchants romanced her with gloves and handkerchiefs and pocketbooks, jewelers sent trinkets, couturiers proffered furs and clothes. Gabrielle "Coco" Chanel, whose fashion salon was directly across from the Cambon doorway, invited her to sample her ready-made racks. "Take what you want," she said, and she did. Claude questioned the gifts but didn't object, although he was incorruptible.

"Bribery is a way of life here," she told him.

"Lucky for you that one doesn't know your real name is Rubenstein," he said in a cryptical reference to Chanel.

She also went with guests to the city's late-night entertainments. Claude allowed it but would not accompany her. He had no liking for cabaret.

He scoffed at the worldwide notion that Paris was a wicked place. Blanche knew why—because he was a recognizable Frenchman, shills never approached him to buy a dirty postcard or visit a brothel. Americans could walk a few paces down a street behind him, and it was as though a sign reading "MADE IN U.S.A." lit up on their chests.

He turned away guests wanting directions to peepshows and sexually explicit circuses, saying they didn't exist. "See here, you must not believe what you hear about this city. Its reputation for sin is undeserved. I have lived most of my life in Paris, and I tell you it is a base canard!"

Once, Blanche hinted she had seen her first such exhibition, but he thought she was making it up as a joke on him. He reproved her, saying, "I will not listen to stories in bad taste." So she didn't report what she saw after that—stark-naked and bare-breasted dancers, nude boys depicting castration ceremonies, girls wriggling madly and sensuously out of chastity belts, a Satanic impersonation of the Dolly Sisters by two notorious homosexuals, the Rocky Twins. In more sedate clubs, featuring artists more fully clothed, she saw Mistinguette, Chevalier, Mellor, and the American rage, Josephine Baker, who replaced Florence Mills when that talented star died during a performance of an "All-Colored Revue" on the Champs-Elysées. "I went with the tourists so often I could do anybody's act backwards. And some would have been better that way."

There were women who thought Blanche danced too well; they didn't ask her twice. But men wanted her along every night of their stay.

After one of those nights, a tall, steely fellow close to sixty sent word to Claude to come to his suite.

"He is a man used to giving orders," Claude told her later. "I could tell by the manner." Then he laughed heartily before adding, "I want you to hear this."

Evans Sheldon's arrival in Paris had been reported in the newspapers. He was meeting with officials of Renault; the possibility of a merger between French and American auto interests was in the columns of *Le Figaro* that day. "I saw at once," said Claude, "he is a man accustomed to getting what he wants."

He loaded cigars and brandy on a desk, invited Claude to help himself, then matter-of-factly described his admiration for Blanche, how she danced, her sense of humor, her beauty . . .

Claude cut him short. "Look here, it is not necessary to tell me these good points about my wife. I know them. I know them better than you."

"Then," chuckled Claude, "this maker of cars shifted gears. He described his home in America, his social position, his wealth, his generosity. I saw then the purpose."

She smiled delightedly. "He wants me!"

"Yes, to marry you! Aha, then you know! He has already told you, eh?"

"No, but it's the way you were when you busted in on J'Ali!"

He nodded.

A flash of humor: "I did it better. I had passion! This American has none. You are another business deal to him. He would buy you like . . . like . . ."

"Like a second-hand car! Did you make the deal? What do I get out of it?"

His humor could go no further. "Look here, it is the last time you will go out. I tell you, it is finished."

She threw herself in his arms, saying, "Oh, Popsy, you are unbelievable! Don't you see how funny it is?"

No, he didn't.

When Franklin D. Roosevelt became President of the United States early in 1933, one of his first acts was to abolish prohibition. Americans in the Ritz Bar celebrated with the same fervor as their fellow drinkers in the speakeasies of New York. It was such a great day that it even penetrated the reserve of British shipping tycoon Sir Harrison Hughes, who bought champagne for everybody and bestowed orchids, for which he had a passion, on all the women. For Blanche, it was the beginning of a beautiful friendship.

However, the world depression continued, and such festive occasions at the Ritz were rare. In June, American heiress Barbara Hutton tried to alleviate some of the pain of empty ballrooms. She celebrated what would be a short-lived marriage to Russian-born Prince Alex Mdivani with a wedding breakfast in the hotel. It cost the Hutton family $25,000.

Later that year, Sir Harrison Hughes, friendly to Claude and charmed by Blanche, offered them a Christmas holiday on one of his freighters. All Harrison Line vessels were cargo carriers. They plied the Mediterranean and through the Atlantic to the Caribbean islands and Gulf ports. Schedules were subject to change with undeclared destinations and unexpected stopovers.

Claude said, "It will be more than a vacation; it will be an adventure."

And it was, but not for him.

As the sailing date neared, waves of violence began to sweep through France. Because of this, Claude elected to stay close to the hotel. Concerned with her safety, however, he wanted her to go without him. There was space on a Harrison Line vessel heading for Martinique and Tampico.

But he didn't want her to be alone.

Maggy Fahmi-Bey, whose liaison with Marshall Hall had come to an end, turned her down. She was leaving for London, she said, "to do some shopping." It had a familiar ring; it was what Blanche had told J'Ali when she saw him in England. "You can put it off," Blanche said coldly, "if that's true."

Friendships in the Ritz, ever fragile, shattered easily. Rather than break the bond between them, Maggy confessed she was going to rendezvous with a new lover. She hinted he was even more formidable than the famous barrister he had replaced.

Blanche had to be satisfied with a promise his identity would be made known to her when she returned.

Pearl White was happy to go along, but Claude wasn't happy with her. "You weren't exactly overjoyed with Maggy either," said Blanche.

"But her melodrama has finished," he growled. "This one lives through a new one every week."

They were shipmates again.

That first afternoon, heading west from Marseilles, they reminded themselves of that earlier voyage. Then, abruptly, their shadows swung around the deck.

The ship was changing course.

From the bridge, the Captain shouted that a sister ship had run aground near Alexandria and he was ordered there to save a perishable cargo.

When the significance of the message sank in, Pearl decided Allah had finally got around to answering J'Ali's prayers. Blanche started for the radio room.

"Why?"

"I have to let Claude know."

"Why?"

Pearl saw the possibility Claude would order Blanche home. That would ruin it for her, too.

"If you must tell someone, send a wireless to J'Ali. Let him give thanks that Allah has finally fixed him up." As for Claude, she voiced a common excuse of the day. "What he doesn't know won't hurt him."

"He's bound to know."

"Let him find out for himself. I never told *my* husbands."

That argument didn't sway her, but Blanche reasoned that Claude couldn't accuse her of planning a rendezvous with J'Ali. It was an act of God, or Allah, or fate. "So I didn't let him

78

know what happened, but then I didn't radio J'Ali either. I wanted the fun of surprising him."

Before she sailed, Sir Harrison Hughes had made it clear to the Captain that he esteemed Claude's character and valued his friendship. Blanche noted that because of that the officers and crew acted as chaperones, which automatically deprived them of anything to chaperone. No other males were aboard.

Pearl got all their amorous attentions. She had a nonstop cocktail party going throughout the voyage. But Blanche, because of the hands-off policy toward her, wasn't even able to partake of the fringe benefits.

By the time they reached port, she was ready for anything J'Ali had to offer.

However, her efforts to find him were unavailing, and his servants wouldn't look for him. After a particularly frustrating call to Cairo, she mimicked a voice that said, "Prince he no like me look him," adding, "That's Egyptian for 'Why-don't-you-get-the-hell-off-the-phone.'"

To reach Claude, she had to wait hours, and then she had to listen to him sputter with rage.

"No problem at all," she told Pearl after she hung up. "He said it's all your fault."

Somehow he attributed their diversion to Pearl's chronic talent for bringing chaos into order.

Their ship was taking the transferred cargo to a remote port on the east coast of Africa. The Captain came to their hotel to invite them along.

"I was very polite," Blanche said. "I waited a full second before telling him he couldn't drag me there."

They were stranded.

The ship that went aground was being towed to drydock for repairs. The only other Harrison Lines vessel that could return them to France wasn't due for three weeks.

At sea, Pearl was free and uninhibited, an extremely pleasant travel partner. Ashore, she was a heavy burden. Hampered by her need for a walking stick, she was reluctant to move around the city. Dust, insects and humid weather bothered her. Beggars with dirty babies repelled her. She complained incessantly.

Hotel employees suggested a variety of amusements, including rides on donkeys, water buffalo and camels. "I couldn't drag Pearl within yards of those beasts," Blanche said. True to herself, she wasn't eager to visit the ancient sites. Three weeks of boredom loomed ahead.

Then J'Ali came roaring up in what was probably the smartest-looking motor car in Egypt, its exterior all shining, its brass headlights as big as lighthouse beacons, blatantly overpowering the rest of the car. He had got the word in Turkey and believed she had left Claude for him. "We had a fantastic reunion, exciting as hell, racing around the desert in his car. I even loved looking at the Pyramids and the Sphynx," Blanche recalled later.

"But the damnedest thing happened. I really was primed to sleep with him, but when we got back to the hotel, he was the one who held back. He wanted me to go right off to Turkey, and we had to wait until we got there. . . . He was furious that I wouldn't go.

"I think he was nervous about his family. I never met any of them, but he was certainly a different fellow at home than when he was abroad. We fought like hell, but I certainly wasn't going to Turkey with him. How would I explain that to Claude?

"So it was J'Ali who loused us up. Back in New York, he didn't give a damn what people thought, but now he was changed. He didn't quite look the same either, although he still dyed his hair. The art of dyeing hair wasn't as precise in Egypt as in Paris or New York. He probably didn't know that there were tufts of grey showing in the back. But that didn't matter—I still liked him. Yes, it really was the damnedest thing, because I would have gone to bed with him in Cairo, but he only wanted to go to bed with me in Constantinople!"

The situation was resolved by the growing thunder of events in France. The country was torn by a full-blown crisis, and that decided her to hurry back to Claude while Pearl stayed on at the hotel to await the returning ship.

ABOVE: Blanche had a
heart-shaped face with
enormous hazel eyes.
(*Courtesy Doris Frankel.*)
RIGHT: Claude had a
small black mustache
and matching eyes.
(*Courtesy Jean Giaume.*)

PRECEDING PAGE: The
hotel Claude admired
most stood at the Place
Vendôme near the
Napoleon monument.
(*Courtesy Air France.*)

LEFT: Her attorney called Maggy Fahmi-Bey "outraged, abused, beaten, degraded." RIGHT: Fahmi-Bey in later years. (*Courtesy Kitty Hemsley.*) BELOW: Her movie producers described Pearl White as "peerless and fearless." She added, "And petrified!" (*Courtesy Miles Kreuger.*)

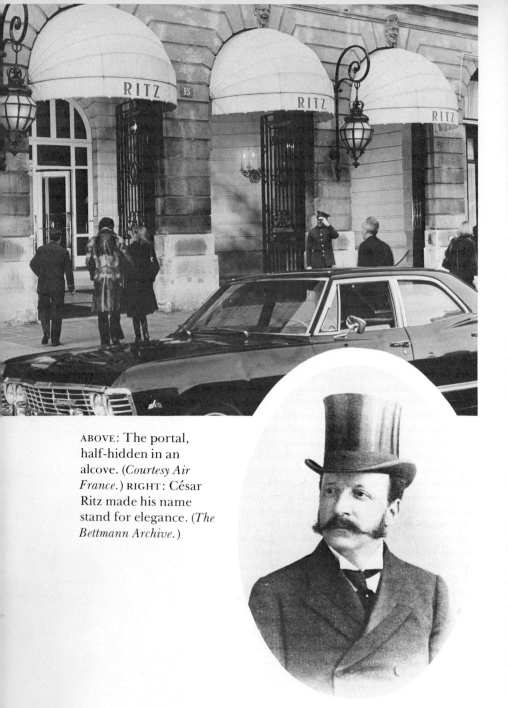

ABOVE: The portal, half-hidden in an alcove. (*Courtesy Air France.*) RIGHT: César Ritz made his name stand for elegance. (*The Bettmann Archive.*)

OPPOSITE, ABOVE: The Ritz terrace—scented with the heady perfume of money. BELOW: Place Vendôme and the Ritz (behind the obelisk), through to the Rue Cambon. (*Photos courtesy Air France.*)

LEFT: Brother Herman joined the musicians' safari to Hollywood. (*Courtesy Betty Ruby.*) BELOW, LEFT: Blanche posed with her parents in fashionable attire. (*Courtesy Carolyn Robbins.*) RIGHT: Claude's father, Joseph, said his son had found an ideal mate. (*Courtesy Francette Combe.*)

ABOVE: "Death was no stranger." Olive Thomas died at the Ritz. LEFT: Her husband, Jack Pickford, also died in Paris. (*Photos courtesy the Museum of Modern Art/Film Stills Archive, 1 West 53rd Street, New York City.*)

ABOVE: "The Dolly
Sisters were
momentarily single."
(*Culver Pictures.*) RIGHT:
Blanche said of "Coco"
Chanel, "There's a lady
I'd like to meet." (*The
Bettmann Archive.*)

"We have lost a great opportunity," J'Ali said as he drove Blanche to the airport, where she was to board a crowded, flimsy, twin-engined plane. "But it is written that we shall be together again, and you will come to see that this is so." Then he gunned the car and left her without an embrace, an indication that he, like her, could control his desires.

The plane, Italian-owned, deposited her in Genoa. There she was told that further flights were canceled, strikes were closing airports throughout France, and rail travel was uncertain. Trains were standing at the frontiers with no indication when they would move.

Worried and impatient, she boarded a small coastal passenger boat that would carry her to a French port.

The uprisings and general strikes that paralyzed France began in January 1934. They were called the Stavisky Riots, in dubious honor of Alexandre Stavisky, an elegant consort of imperial politicians and lovely women, both of whom he wooed with equal intensity.

Who this attractive Russian was and what he did were mysterious puzzles of crooked finance. For years he had made his headquarters at the Claridge, where he had planned some of the niftiest swindles in the history of France.

Claude knew him only by sight then; Stavisky wasn't the type to deal with an assistant manager. He cashed a worthless check on M. Marquet. The enraged hotel owner threatened jail, but relented when the money was repaid.

Stavisky then passed another bad check. That victim was nightclub owner Joe Zelli, who had him arrested. Such were the minor beginnings of the man who came dangerously close to tumbling a great nation.

After a brief stay in jail and a "provisional" release, he moved up to higher grades of fraud, embezzlement and other miscellaneous illegalities. Claude moved from the Claridge while Stavisky's activities pyramided. When Claude came to know him, he was giving huge receptions at the Ritz for France's greatest statesmen.

In her autobiography, Colette told of observing him in 1934, "a slender figure in the corridors and rooms of the Ritz."

He was nearly fifty, she wrote, and wore a light though detectable layer of makeup—cream and powder—in an attempt to retain his youthful appearance. She saw in this the long periods spent in front of a mirror, the lucid study of a declining face, the secret struggle against advancing age.

"He was in the tiny barber shop at the Ritz for haircuts and manicures, constantly turning himself this way and that, to closely observe his features, looking for . . . what? To see if others might see in him the man he alone knew to be there?"

Through a curious twist of fate tied to Blanche's trip to Egypt, the scandals that enveloped the adventurer brought about Claude's promotion to the post he had always dreamed of holding at the Ritz.

Blanche struck up an acquaintance aboard the little boat with a small, dark girl, Lily Kharmayeff, a bundle of quirks and unpredictability, exactly the sort of character who would intrigue Blanche. A stateless person, living entirely by her wits, Lily had fled tyranny in many countries of Eastern Europe, yet was utterly at ease with the world, frank, devious when necessary, but childishly happy to have managed a temporary visa to France, where she planned to remain. Permanently.

Her hair flying wild, a trace of slant to her lozenge-shaped eyes, she claimed to be directly descended from Genghis Khan, the Mongol-Turkish nomad who ruled the tribes of antiquity. Blanche listened to the chatter of her new friend tolerantly, and with enjoyment.

"You and me, we write my book about my *ancien*, Genghis Khan, yes?" said Lily, who had a habit of recruiting people into her endeavors without asking how they felt about it. "I have all the true story. You will make millions of dollars, and I will star when they do in cinema."

During the voyage, she passed on varying observations of the men she had known. All were "no-goodnicks. All Italians, they say me I cannot resist them. You say me about all Frenchmen and American mens and I will probably sleep with many, but I make the choice, yes?" She seriously advised Blanche to avoid Egyptians. All time fock, no give fun."

The boat steamed into Marseilles on a cold, bleak February dawn; the crew tied it up to a deserted pier, then vanished. The few passengers waited, expecting immigration authorities to come aboard and give them permission to land. All but Lily.

She darted down the gangplank, astounded that the entrance to France was unpatrolled, saying that if she had known how easy it "be me" to walk into France, she could have saved herself all the waiting she encountered getting a visa.

Telephones were out, telegrams refused, with Claude nearly eight hundred kilometers away. Blanche finally lugged her makeup kit and one valise off the boat and was starting off uncertainly when Lily returned.

She had hired a beat-up Citroen to take them to Paris. "I says him you are rich American lady or I no get," she explained. "You pay hundred dollars, U.S.A. Good, yes?"

Blanche retrieved an abandoned valise and then recruited a middle-aged passenger who agreed to pay half the fare for a ride to his home along the way.

The driver, a surly Algerian, demanded another hundred when he discovered he was transporting more than he had bargained for, but Lily, taking over as leader of the expedition, engaged him in a savage harangue and he backed down. Thoroughly intimidated, he glowered at her, while she told Blanche, "Naturally, he likes me very much."

They took off with the car sagging with their weight, the luggage tied precariously on top, and an auxiliary can containing 15,000 hectoliters of petrol inside, procured by the driver from a fellow Algerian at the cost of Blanche's last franc.

The extra passenger proved more disagreeable than the Algerian. Cramped in the front between driver and petrol can, he was outraged when he found he was paying half, argued that he should pay a third or less. Arguments went on during the whole of the long, cold, uncomfortable day, until Blanche asked how he happened to be carrying American currency. He snapped his teeth together and refused to answer, but neither did he continue the argument.

He left them at a small farmhouse, set in a brown field a few miles outside of Lyon. They were hardly back on the highway when a hard rain began to pelt down. The driver pulled off the road and announced, reasonably enough, it was as far as he would go without a rest. In Lyon he located some petrol and paid for it when Blanche swore it would be returned to him in Paris.

With the two women hugging each other for warmth, they drove on, Paris still a day and a half away, their nerves frayed to the breaking point. Blanche relaxed when familiar landmarks appeared, but not for long. They had hardly reached the outer city when mobs, in cars and on foot, jammed the streets. All were inching toward the Place de la Bastille, directly between them and the Ritz. It was February 6. The wheels of the city had halted, all its daily activities at a standstill. Shops and business offices were closed. Even those who had sworn to uphold the law were off their jobs.

It was all the result of the uncovering of Stavisky's greatest fraud. He had set himself up to sell municipal bonds for the city of Bayonne, which seemed to the man in the street secure investments, backed as they were by the assets of government-owned pawnshops.

Actually, each legitimate bond had an identical twin with the same number printed on it. The money paid for one went to the treasury of Bayonne, but the money paid for the duplicate went to Stavisky.

The scheme came to light late in 1933. The victims proved to be ordinary workmen, members of labor unions. By that time, they had been cheated out of over eighteen million dollars. It was inconceivable that Stavisky could have put across such a swindle without the help of high-placed officials. He disappeared and was reported to have committed suicide, whereupon the wrath of the victims turned against senators, deputies and police. Violent eruptions ensued, and fifteen people died when the workers mobbed the Chamber of Deputies.

84

Trying to outflank the crowds, Blanche and company drove through narrow alleys. In a short time, the driver was hopelessly lost. Blanche couldn't tell if they were getting closer to the Ritz or moving away from it.

The luggage on top and the women inside made the machine an obvious target for unruly youths looking for trouble. Suddenly, the driver pulled over to the curb and ordered Blanche and Lily out. He folded his arms, looked straight ahead, and waited for them to get out.

At the hotel, strikers were solidly massed, surrounding it. Nobody could get in or out. There was no service; guests were keeping to their rooms or huddled in the salons. On the first floor, the executive staff assembled, looking out through the high windows to the Place Vendôme, commanders of a city under siege.

Colonel Pfyffer, in dress uniform, decided he would handle the situation. He took one step out of the front door and shouted to the massed strikers and pickets to disperse.

His words and waving arms brought roars of laughter. First they hurled obscenities at him, but then their hostility took a more dangerous turn and stones were added to the jeers. A rock narrowly missed his face, crashed into the glass door behind him. Another roar, louder than before, completely unnerved him, and he scrambled back inside.

The high command was helpless. During the shocked silence that greeted the Colonel's retreat, Claude saw Blanche on the far side of the Place Vendôme, bedraggled, unable to get through to the hotel's entrance. He ran down the staircase. A girl secretary was near the foot of it, and he beckoned to her. "You! Come with me!"

She followed him out the door, to be greeted with jeers and catcalls. The leader of the strikers pointed to him and warned him to go back inside or suffer bodily harm.

At this, Claude whipped off his coat and handed it to the girl. He rolled up his sleeves and strode toward Blanche. He wasn't as big as the man who barred his way, but what he lacked in size he made up in pugnacity.

He thrust his fist in the man's face and said, hoarsely, *"Vous me laissez passer . . . ou je vous casse la gueule!"* The man backed away from him. So did men immediately behind him. Then Claude swung past, forcing everyone in his path to step aside by sheer force of belligerency.

When he got to Blanche, he put his arms around her and kissed her. Then he took her makeup kit, which was all she still had of her luggage, and escorted her through the crowd and into the hotel.

When she was inside, he strode back to the curb. Every eye was on him.

"Allez!" he commanded. *"TOUS!"*

They ran. The secretary held out his coat, and he donned it, smiling at her and at the awed expressions of his associates who rushed out to acclaim him. (Charley Ritz, who disapproved of the strict sartorial rules that Claude enforced on guests of the hotel, later said, "That has to be the only time anyone ever saw Claude Auzello in his shirtsleeves, but understand, it was only outside and he was in correct attire before reentering the hotel!")

Later that day, Marie Louise summoned him. His exploit had swept through Paris; high-ranking government officials called to ask his name. "You saved the hotel," she said.

It was the only one in Paris that was functioning. Those employees who were inside resumed their duties. Others who had walked out returned. At the next meeting of the board, she would recommend he be made Managing Directeur.

Victor Rey assured him he could take that to be an accomplished fact. Baron Pfyffer, who had been standing silently behind Marie Louise, came forward and shook his hand.

Blanche had gone straight to bed, but he shook her and woke her with a kiss. As she rubbed her eyes, trying to banish the immediate need of sleep, she heard him telling his father over the phone in Nice, "I have been chosen to fill the shoes of César Ritz!"

8

"Three hundred years from now the name Ritz will still have meaning everywhere in the world."
—Marie Louise Ritz

The troubles, that fashionable understatement of the times, brought a dapper expatriate home. Charley Ritz bounced in on Claude soon after he arrived in France.

He was older than Claude, small and peppery, thin, spry and sardonic. He enjoyed talking in epigrams. He was pro-American, pro-German and anti-French. He had come to explain his position in the operation of the hotel. He wanted no part of it.

His consuming passion in life was fly fishing, and he was on his way to becoming an authority on the subject. He was working on what he hoped would be the definitive book about it. Among the tips he offered his readers were the following:

Look out for ricocheting bullets in the hunting season.

Any report on salmon fishing in Norway would be incomplete if it made no mention of the summer plague, mosquitoes. A peculiar native device for protecting oneself when fishing from one of the countless lakes in Lapland consists of recruiting a couple of Lapp women, between whom one stands and who attract the insects which have a preference for strong scents.

In order to be free to cast his line at will around the world, he was defying the wishes of his mother, who wanted him involved with running the Ritz.

But he was always reluctant to be part of the hotel business, although at twenty-one he had worked briefly at the Hotel

87

Mohican in New London, Connecticut. His admiration for life in the United States was great; his Americanization began the day he started on the job wearing a swallow-tail coat and was told, "This is a hotel, not an undertaking parlor."

He enlisted in the American army during World War I, although he was Swiss and not obligated. He was in uniform when his father died in 1918. Then, after the war, he went fishing again, making only sporadic visits to France on his way to European waters. He often brought along his American wife, Betty.

Always direct, facile and persuasive, Charley convinced his mother he shouldn't join the staff. As a compromise, he agreed to stay on in Paris. He preferred to take a job as a customer's man with an American brokerage firm. His meeting with Claude was to tell him of this decision.

Claude told him he would be pleased if he changed his mind.

"But I don't agree with your policies. I would only make problems for you. I don't respect traditions."

"Even those of your father?"

"No. I don't subscribe to the idea that if it's old it must be good. My mother, of course, feels as you do. I am the only one who realizes my father has been dead sixteen years. It is time we buried him."

From then on, although Claude understood and knew the history of Charley Ritz almost as intimately as he did César's, Claude would have trouble with Charley.

César Ritz had called the hotel his daughter. "My most beautiful child," he said. He loved her more than he did his sons, but they didn't care much for him, either. To Claude, Charley candidly said, "Why should I care for a stranger? My father hardly knew me from the time I was a little boy."

César Ritz traveled so widely that he left Charley practically fatherless, and when he got around to him it was too late to innoculate him with a love for hotels. The lonesome little boy had found what he wanted in the solitude and suspense that were his when he fished in the lakes and streams near his home in Switzerland. No pleasures compared to landing graylings and salmon on a slim reed. When the flapping, gasping foe was lying at his feet, he would dance on the bank with his good-luck alpine hat tilted cockily askew and give a lung-bursting yodel. They were his moments of triumph. He couldn't have them in a luxury hotel, especially the Ritz.

He carried his tackle wherever the fish were large and elusive, feeling challenged to go after them. He compared the fight and the victory to a battle for survival in a bull ring. He would cross oceans to meet a champion, and once, unbelievable but true, he went after a great shark and landed it on a flypole.

On another occasion, he took his wife Betty to Labrador, where the salmon were fantastic fighters. They made an arduous journey into the wilderness via pack trails and canoes, camping at an Indian settlement on the Romaine, near the Arctic Circle.

The approach of winter weather made it necessary to limit their time and get out. Meanwhile, he caught a meager six, while she landed eighteen, one a record-breaking monster. For that, she was adopted by the tribe in a wild torch-lit dance. She never went fishing again. He didn't ask her.

Blanche and Betty hit it off magically. They loved the daily social doings in the hotel, were invited by all the party givers, and literally lapped up a bonus in wines and cocktails that were stacked before them on the terrace every afternoon by men who believed that was a way to curry favors from Charley and Claude. These gift drinks stopped coming in the late afternoon after the men moved into the bar, and that triggered their determination to break down the barrier of segregation.

Their efforts were not accepted happily. Claude was on a short fuse; he was overworking, to keep up not just with the routines of his new position but with the responsibilities he added to them himself. He was further annoyed by Charley Ritz's insinuations that Blanche was responsible for Betty's drinking problem. He refused to open the Cambon Bar to them, reminding Blanche its male exclusivity was in the César Ritz tradition. He expected her to know better than to change that.

Protocol demanded that someone fill the position of manager that he was giving up. Meticulously, he delved into the backgrounds of the men in contention. Hans Elmiger was a natural choice, having climbed upward through years of service in numerous departments. Charming, self-effacing, knowledgeable, he had one possible drawback: he was Baron Pfyffer's nephew.

Checking his record, Claude discovered that when Elmiger had worked as a cashier there were discrepancies in accounts and considerable money was missing. All seven workers in that department were suspect, but Victor Rey discovered and proved that Elmiger was the only one who checked out as honest. The others were fired. "If he were not related to the Baron," Claude told Blanche, "I would choose him automatically. I assure you, I will not cater to that old man."

He was still undecided when the entire staff assembled in the grand ballroom, at the invitation of Marie Louise, to hear what they already knew. Claude Auzello was the hotel's new Managing Directeur.

Whatever suspense there was had to be the identity of the man who would replace him as manager.

In his address, Claude said, "The excellence César Ritz wished to achieve requires vigilance and hard work, the kind that distinguishes the illustrious—yes, the genius—from the common laborer. I am no genius—I most certainly am not—but I promise hard work, friendliness and hospitality as the qualities that will set our hotel apart."

He informed them he would make regular inspections of the outfits they wore and warned the concierges that their blue and gold uniforms must be spotless to impress arriving guests. As a former army officer, he was no stranger to daily inspections. "However," he said with a flash of humor that was greeted by cheers and applause, "I shall not ask you to parade at dawn!"

He warned the captains of all departments that they had to promote honesty and sobriety and see that those working under them took no offense from real or fancied insults.

"I am forced to say to you that when complaints are made, I

shall side with the guest. That is our policy, and there will be no exceptions."

Then, deliberately slowly, he spoke of the need of a second in command and, smilingly, asked Hans Elmiger to accept that position. He was a popular choice; the respect of his co-workers was evident. As Claude moved to shake his hand, the Baron grabbed Claude by the shoulders and embraced him. Some of the antagonism between the Baron and the Auzellos ended there, but not all. "I didn't mind his hugging you," Blanche told Claude, "but if he tried to kiss you I would have hit him with a chair."

Before they all went back to work, Claude paid tribute to Blanche and expressed gratitude to the Ritz family. Then he rushed away to his new office, just off the Vendôme lobby. It had been a writing room for guests until he appropriated it and hung a sign PRIVATE on the door.

The rapport he hoped to achieve with the staff was going to take time. Union problems intruded immediately. The demands of labor, often backed by the government, seemed designed just to create discord for him. Soon after he settled into his office, a delegation of window-washers informed him that henceforth they would perform their duties only from inside. Others would wash the outside—younger men who enjoyed balancing themselves on windowsills. But because of the risk involved, they wanted more money. The "inside" group, having seniority, wanted more, too.

He supervised the itemizing of every scrap of linen from napkins to sheets, every piece of silver, the wine, the contents of storerooms long left unattended, the furniture throughout, including that in rooms and suites, and he catalogued the seeds and blooms and everything growing in the flower and vegetable gardens. Abhorrent of cold-storage foods, he demanded that all meats, fruits and vegetables be brought fresh to the Ritz kitchen. He ordered the inventory be kept up-to-date, a difficult accomplishment because even the most elite guest was likely to assume the ownership of spoons, ashtrays and towels. He kept the list, growing to encyclopedic size, locked in his office.

91

He woke Blanche up one morning, meaning only to bend over her with a kiss. It was dawn; he was fully dressed and leaving for Les Halles.

Workers around the big open-air market were astounded to see the head man ride in on the Ritz truck. He sampled fruits and vegetables, squeezing, tasting, spitting out items of inferior quality, forcing farmers and vendors to accept prices he considered fair. The know-how picked up around his father's market in Monte Carlo was paying off; he knew the quality of meats and what he wanted and would only settle for the best.

His visits to Les Halles became regular routine. When the news spread, other hotel men appeared, but their knowledge of what to buy was limited. The profession's seven-day week brought them out tired and complaining. Their appearances stopped altogether in a few weeks, but Claude went on.

Being committed to operating the hotel as César Ritz believed it should be, he was also unceasing in his wish that it be admired by all. Its reputation was of supreme importance.

"I do not expect to know everything," he told Blanche. "But I attempt it."

Driving away in a taxicab, he assumed the character of a tourist and asked, "Is it a good hotel, the Ritz?"

"*Oui, monsieur*. The best."

"I can take chicks to my room there?"

"Probably" was the hearty answer. "First try giving ten francs to the Managing Directeur!"

He told Blanche, "Look here, that is a joke on me, is it not? I see its humor. I am not so foolish as to think sex can be stamped out."

"*Voilà!*" she said. "Claude Auzello grows up at last!"

"Look here, it is not sex that I object to."

"Why should you? Wasn't it invented in France?"

"It is vulgarity that I cannot allow in the Ritz."

Knowing her love of gossip, he was willing to tell her stories that came to his attention, but in spite of her pleadings, he usually withheld names. "Hotel men who cannot learn to be discreet would be wise to learn another profession," he said. "And quickly!"

One must never ask about an absent wife or husband, he noted. Just the previous weekend, he had shown a room to a visiting British diplomat and his lady, who would be overnight guests. She was an attractive blonde, with the fresh peach-bloom complexion of the English. "That," he said, "was all I really noticed about her."

Two nights later, he noticed a couple in the restaurant, and it puzzled him that the woman kept looking keenly at him. When the man left her for a few minutes, she rushed over and said, "Thank you for not greeting me, Mr. Auzello. You see how awkward it would be, because the man I met you with the other day is a very dear friend, but this one is my husband."

Chuckling, he said to Blanche, "The truth is, I didn't recognize her as the one who checked in with the diplomatic fellow. But if I had, I would not have indicated it. She had nothing to worry about."

His anecdotes often concerned less romantic matters. One morning a maid discovered a man in bed who was thought dead but turned out to be drunk. A few hours later, a man thought to be drunk turned out to be dead.

The routine machinery, established long before Claude ascended to the top position, went into gear. The coroner certified death due to natural causes, the family—well known in the area of Rouen—was notified, and an undertaker was sent on his way. Meanwhile the body was placed in a wicker basket and crowded in with other storage items near the service exit. It was moved furtively through deserted corridors. The hotel tried to keep customers from seeing any aspects of death.

Unfortunately, the undertaker's hearse broke down on the road, and Claude was advised it could not reach Paris until after midnight. The storage area would be padlocked for the night. What did he want done with the body until it was picked up?

There was no function booked in the ballroom that night, and he ordered it placed there until the undertaker showed up. But the undertaker never arrived, and in the morning an elaborate wedding ceremony took place in the ballroom, with breakfast following. Two hundred celebrants were blissfully unaware they had a corpse behind a curtain at a window close to the bride and groom and their receiving line.

"I stationed a bellhop near the curtain, prepared to stop anyone who might want to open the window, but no one did, although I still tremble at the thought of what might have happened," said Claude. As soon as the wedding guests departed, the body was hustled out of the hotel.

Twelve years after his wife, Olive Thomas, passed away at the hotel in a haze of mystery, Jack Pickford became deathly ill at the hotel and was hurried off to the American Hospital, where he died. Claude was grateful he hadn't passed away at the Ritz.

"Poor fellow," said Claude. "Too much women, drink and riotous living."

"All the right things," observed Blanche.

Blanche finally won her campaign to break down the barrier against women in the Cambon Bar. It was a popular victory. Clusters of males celebrated their entrance with cheers and ribald toasts.

Every day thereafter, when the bar opened, Frank Meier tipped a half-dozen chairs against a wall table. He held it especially for her and the friends she invited to sit there.

The easy availability of liquor worried Claude. To appease him, Blanche arranged to signal the bartenders with a rippling finger on the right hand for scotch and on the left for a look-alike ginger ale. She wanted the others at the table to think she was matching them drink for drink. But the real scotches outnumbered the make-believe, and those convivial afternoons provoked Charley Ritz.

"Your wife is turning mine into an alcoholic," he told Claude. That split the two men further apart; Claude believed the exact opposite was true. But Blanche and Betty Ritz went on as friendly as ever.

They especially enjoyed the important status that was theirs, not only with the personnel but also in the eyes of the hotel guests. Although she was not yet familiar with the workers in the bar, Blanche felt that her prestige demanded that she know them all by their first names. She accomplished that by asking the waiters and busboys who were strangers to her to respond when she called "Jean-Pierre."

The presence of four huge brass spittoons offended both women. It sparked a new campaign to get rid of them. The men who were regulars in the bar took a stand, saying, in effect, there-goes-the-neighborhood. The management—represented by Claude—decreed that the spittoons would stay.

One day at the bar, Broadway playwright Moss Hart brought Cole Porter a gift of gold garters. The composer said, "Just what I need," pulled up his trousers, took off identical gold garters, replaced them with the new, then tossed the discarded pair into one of the spittoons.

Describing the incident to Claude, Blanche said, "Nobody spits in the Ritz." It wasn't much of an argument, but it was enough, and the spittoons were removed.

She could win against Claude, but others could not.

Moineau was an actress in Sascha Guitry's company, a gaudy creature reputed to have once been a flower girl. Her name, in English, translated as *Sparrow*, and that was how she was popularly known.

She had a millionaire husband who spent much of his time on his yacht at Cannes, while she preferred Paris, where she gave rowdy parties and figured in several café-society scandals. One Sunday afternoon she had a table for twenty reserved for lunch on the terrace.

Her guests were mostly gigolos, along with several notorious hangers-on, a collection that alerted Claude's attention even before Moineau arrived. She made her entrance wearing a yachting cap and a man's suit with plaid trousers.

Any flaunting of conventional dress outraged Claude. He informed Moineau she could not be seated until she changed costume, and when she defied him he ordered the waiters not to serve her. The entire party walked out, vowing never to return.

Alexander Kingsley (King) Macomber and his wife, Standard Oil heiress Myrtle Harkness, were two of the greatest eccentrics among Ritz guests. They were also among its wealthiest, for between them they owned Catalina Island (before Wrigley), much of Pasadena, hunting lodges around Europe and America, and a racing stable of champions. Both had a horror of photographers, which made them a special target of newspaper and magazine cameramen. An American news syndicate offered to give the Ritz free publicity and advertising for three years if Claude would allow a photographer to take secret, candid shots of the couple from behind curtains. Claude personally escorted the man through the exit, then reported the incident to the Board of Directors.

Charley Ritz told his mother, "He runs the hotel like it's his private club." But Marie Louise thoroughly approved; it was what César would have done.

The passions generated by Alexandre Stavisky died away. The swindler, too, was dead; no one could reliably say if he shot himself or was shot by police when they closed in on his hideout at Chamonix. The troubles apparently past, France and the Ritz settled down to their accustomed grandeur again.

Blanche had one friend who could not relate to it. She invited Lily Kharmayeff to the bar, but the girl, ill at ease and incongruous in "my ensemble," put together with red shoes and hair dyed to match, stayed only a few minutes. "From now on," she told Blanche, "you come see me, and maybe some day, I says me, I will like this life here. But it is not for now, if you see what I see is happening. In Germany, in Russia, yes, is also in Spain. Then, more, you will say me, Lily is right. I worry. I worry for the whole world."

She was living in a room in an alley across the Boulevard des Capucines. Blanche climbed a steep set of narrow stairs to visit her and was introduced to a set of exotic strangers. The talk was obscure, political and argumentative. Opinions differed, but Lily controlled them, kept them in a low key, subdued by Blanche's presence. Blanche went several times. The atmosphere was always the same.

"It wasn't the kind of talk I was used to, and I was never comfortable. But I kept going back because I loved Lily."

It would be four more years before she would come to realize that Lily did know more about what was going on in the world than all the intellects and diplomats in the Ritz.

Meanwhile she urged Louis Bromfield and Ernest Hemingway to consider Lily as a character for one of their stories, but they put off meeting her, although they were intrigued by Blanche's delightful mimicry of her friend. Bromfield was already mapping out a book about the hotel; it would be fiction, which was his forte, mingled with fact. The heroine he planned to create was a madcap from middle-class America propelled into the luxury of the Ritz, a composite culled from interviews with Blanche and his stately friend, Mrs. Edith Wharton. The poet-novelist had adopted a half-dozen orphans after World War I, raising them on her farm near Senlis, neighboring that of Bromfield.

A meticulous researcher, Bromfield compiled information on Marie Louise Ritz, as well as on the majordomos of the restaurant, the grill, the kitchen and the bar. "I have a feeling nothing short of the end of the world can change what goes on here," he said, writing phrases and philosophies into his notebook. "Wars, revolutions can come and go, but nothing will disturb the perfection of the Ritz."

Resembling a successful American businessman, Bromfield was as deliberate and organized as Hemingway was not. Hemingway, too, intended to write a story about the hotel and told Blanche she would be one of its principal characters. "He thinks it's a way of paying for his drinks," she told Claude. He was friendly, too, with Charley Ritz, whose fishing exploits he envied, and with other characters in the hotel, "the dead bartenders and all the high-class whores I have known." He wanted Blanche to fill him in on the "inside gen" of her life. "Gen" derived from genuine; it was a word he used in conversation. He used it often, as he used "true" in his writing. "Gen" and "true" meant the same to him. But they met only a few times at her table in the bar; he was too restless to stay in Paris for long. The world's growing turmoil diverted him from the story he intended to write.

"The handsomest writer in the world" was how Blanche

described Hemingway's friend, rival and sometime enemy, F. Scott Fitzgerald. He, too, was fascinated by the elegance of the Ritz and would rarely refer to any other hotel in his stories.

He was no favorite of Claude, who considered him a male counterpart of Pearl White. He disliked seeing him in the bar, where he was an unpredictable nuisance, upsetting tables and drinks and the tempers of more rational customers. On one occasion, Blanche took him upstairs to her rooms to sleep off an overindulgence.

"When he woke up, he thought Claude had given him the room, so he went to his office to thank him. I could have killed him, because I didn't want Claude to know. But besides being handsome, Scott was the politest writer I ever knew."

"Claude accepted his thanks without knowing what he was talking about. When he found out, I caught hell."

A writer of a different type of material, charming and talented Cole Porter, used his button-bright eyes to survey all that went on in the bar, for he, too, was fascinated by life in the Ritz. He appeared punctually every morning as soon as it was open, to sit at the same corner table and work on his songs.

Left-handed, with manuscript paper in a vertical position, he penned words and music from the bottom up, his arm twisted around the tabletop. The names of Paris hotels were always finding their way into his lyrical output. Blanche knew one from a song she heard at *La Revue des Ambassadeurs*:

> *That building there upon the right*
> *Is the famous Hotel Claridge.*
> *It's where the ladies go at night*
> *When they're fed up with marriage.*

He sang "Let's Do It" to her while he was working on it:

> *The world admits*
> *Even bears in pits do it—*
> *Even pekineses in the Ritz do it.*
> *Let's do it, let's fall in love.*

Charley Ritz left Paris again, taking Betty with him. He had lost his temper several times when he found her tipsy in the bar, and directed some of his wrath at Blanche, which only widened the gap between him and Claude. Charley's attitude toward Blanche had no effect on her liking for him. He amused her. "A little man who talks big but thinks small," she said. Despite his constant putdowns of his wife, he noted in his book a similarity between women and fly rods: "When maltreated, they won't play."

With Betty's departure, Blanche became sole hostess of the long table at the far end of the bar. The regulars paid court—kissed her hand when they came in, bestowed compliments, relayed the latest gossip, told sultry stories, laughed a lot, and then kissed her hand again as they went out. Not everyone in the bar knew who she was, but those who didn't wondered. Blanche watched as, behind hand-cupped lips, strangers murmured to waiters, their eyes betraying the object of their furtive question. She loved every nuance of attention.

From where she sat, with the entrance directly in her line of vision, no man or woman eluded her appraising eye, whether friend or stranger. Interestingly enough, it wasn't the liquor that was habit-forming, but the manner of living with liquor; the conviviality and congeniality got to her. She was developing a love for hotel life to match that of Claude. She wanted it to go on forever.

One afternoon, Maggy Fahmi-Bey advanced on her table excitedly. "He is here!" she said. "He asks you to dine with us. We shall go dancing. He is a wonderful dancer."

Blanche still didn't know who he was; Maggy had steadfastly concealed her lover's identity.

That evening, Blanche was waiting in the Vendôme doorway when Maggy arrived with him in a long black limousine. He was Edward, Prince of Wales, the intended future King of England.

The Prince's personal equerry was along to make the foursome complete. It was expected that Blanche's presence would soften gossip about them. She was along as a front, a disguise, an alibi, a "mustache"!

"I told Edward not to worry; nobody in Paris gives a damn—Maggy and I could pass for a couple of hookers, and nobody over here will think anything of it."

They were dancing together then, and she made him laugh.

"When I was a girl in New York," she told him, "I remember how envious I was of those classy people I saw going into the best places. I would have given anything to be one of them. I still don't believe it."

The foursome ventured into Paris night life a few more times, and then Edward discovered the American divorcee, Wallis Simpson.

Blanche told Claude, "Poor Maggy. Her big affair is history now. Yes, it sure as hell is history. My kind of history!"

In the spring of 1936, Claude's father died. Seventy-five-year-old Joseph Auzello was buried on a high hill over Nice in the Cimitière St. Roch, beside ancestors who had lain in that setting more than a century.

There were corroding markers, religious statues and elaborate granite edifices that housed the more affluent dead. The snow-capped pinnacles of the Maritime Alps towered in the distance, while the white roofs of the city of Nice and the brilliant blue of the Mediterranean stretched off and away, directly below. The eternal paradox of death and beauty was around them. During the church and graveside ceremonies, Blanche was unable to console her inconsolable husband. His floral offering read, "I have lost the only friend I have in the world."

Claude's youth seemed to pass away with his father. He was preoccupied with the perils of aging and brooded as they drove back to Paris. "Death is a determined companion, and sooner or later makes the acquaintance of us all."

Blanche, trying to shake him out of the mood, said, "If he comes looking for me, just say I'm out and you don't know when I'll be back."

When sprightliness failed, she switched to talk of a subject dear to her heart, the need to live closer to the hotel, a swank apartment in a highly desirable neighborhood.

100

"You are beoming a snob," he growled.

True, she admitted it. All members of the socially prominent were snobs, and she circulated in their company—girls
who sought to marry into royalty, women who desperately
desired to be known as the best-dressed, ladies who gloated
over their husbands' power in finance and politics. Endless
examples passed before her at the Ritz. It was neither original
nor unworthy, she told him, to be a snob. They outnumbered
all his other customers. "Watch how everyone hates to sit in
the rear of the restaurants."

Catering to snobbery was paying off handsomely for the
newest darling of American society in Paris. Sophistication,
beauty and extreme good taste provided only some of the
appeal of chic, magnetic former actress Elsie de Wolfe. Just
before Blanche departed for the funeral of Joseph Auzello,
Elsie said to her, "There is one infallible way to find an apartment in Paris, my dear. Watch the obituaries."

Happily for Blanche, Claude agreed that a change of scene,
a new place for them to live did interest him and he would
welcome it. Before they drove into Passy, he was actually
enthusiastic about it. "I guess he suddenly realized we were in
danger of being old stick-in-the-muds. It was the aftermath to
losing his father. The proximity to death made him reckless.
Or careless. I don't know which, but it was lucky for me."

The tip provided by Elsie de Wolfe paid off.

It was a macabre pastime, poring through the names of the
dead, trying to judge their affluence, and seeking their ad-
dresses in the directories. But that was how she found it.

The heirs were eager for a sale in order to sidestep legal
delays in settling the estate. The body was barely out of the
fourth-floor apartment at 36, Avenue Montaigne when
Blanche toured through. From the balcony she could see the
smart couturiers and millinery shops below; in the distance
the white moonlike top of Sacré-Coeur was dazzling on the hill
of Montmartre. She waved off Claude's qualms about the
speed of her purchase, and he went along, telling his associates, "She holds to principles that our laws are to be observed
only if they are to her advantage."

Elsie de Wolfe was on hand the day Blanche took over the premises, coming from her Villa Trianon outside of Paris, where the decor was striking and sensational. Appeals from the less artistically inclined, willing to pay for her ideas, had made her the world's first interior decorator.

But the concept that his home should be furnished by an outsider brought howls from Claude, "See here, I will not be contaminated by the tastes of others," he said. He branded interior decorating as a ridiculous and temporary vogue and, worse, an unnecessary extravagance.

Blanche, hoping to change his mind, brought Elsie to see him in his office. She suggested a dazzling array of lamps, mirrors, ornaments and zebra skins. But Claude remained undazzled, his mind unchangeable, unmoved by her vision of an "elegant but simple effect."

His attitude toward the modern art she proposed was similar to his attitude toward painters, few of whom went to the Ritz twice, because as far back as César their dress was considered outlandish—it set them apart from the desired clientele. Green velvet jackets and red berets were met at the door with open disapproval, although not barred. It was made obvious that artists were looked upon as characters mistakenly strayed from Montmartre or Montparnasse, and the sooner they returned, the better. Several artists who could afford Ritz prices, Picasso, Derain, Braque and Matisse, resented it and went elsewhere for their cognac.

Perhaps, if it had been otherwise, Claude might have appreciated modern art. However, he rejected the trailblazers and, instead, covered the apartment walls with hunting scenes by painters who would be forever known as Anonymous. Furnishing his way, he stuffed their rooms with baroque furniture, ornate but comfortable.

"I make the decisions," Claude told Blanche, "because I am entirely logical."

"I am married to a stubborn fool," she said, and had to settle for a partial victory.

She was resident in a most elegant neighborhood, with the

finest fashion houses spread out before her front door, from America (Mainbocher), Greece (Jean Desses), Spain (Balenciaga), Italy (Carven), England (Molyneaux), and, of course, France (Balmain, Larouch, Rochas, Worth, Paquin, Lanvin, Poiret, Vionnet, Patou and Lucien Lelong). In a few years, much of the street beneath her window would be occupied by the establishment of young Christian Dior, whose father told him, "At your age, I was more interested in *undressing* women!"

"You should have a crest inscribed 'La Joie de Rien Faire,' " said Maggy Fahmi-Bey.

There were additional advantages derived from marriage to a man running a luxury hotel. When Blanche chose evenings at home, the hotel delivered dinner from its five-star kitchen. Her household linen was cleaned in the hotel's laundry. Claude's suits were pressed by the valet; extra silver service, glassware, linens and floral decorations for parties were rushed to her when she needed them. She received new books from the woman who ran the pavilion for reading matter in the *galerie*, keeping her up on the best sellers in the United States, always an important conversational gambit with new arrivals.

Meanwhile the depression was sliding by, but the moneyed set continued to live in the manner to which it was accustomed.

The price for their luxuries came high, with ten percent on top for service. Americans, mostly, called compulsory tipping a pernicious habit. Europeans were programmed to expect the personnel to want more, to stand on a smiling receiving line with hands outstretched, palms upward.

A prominent Parisienne died, scattering her money to more than fifty heirs. "She departed this world like she was checking out of the Ritz" was the comment in the bar.

In the beginning, Blanche criticized the practice, especially when she discovered that the hotel used the tipping custom as an excuse to pay lower salaries.

Claude saw nothing wrong with that. "The rich get satisfaction out of giving. See here, it is a psychological thing. Tipping adds to the joy of being rich."

As time went on, she grew to accept the practice. Her education into the world of rosewood and sophistication, velvet curtains and silken charm had too much dream quality to fight against; it was beautifully unreal, all glitter and glamour. Even with some of the real world tottering and tumbling, people in the Ritz lived for themselves alone, and, as Blanche now realized, Claude knew exactly how to cater to them and how to chastise them, too. It was all unbelievably attractive.

Smoothly and with precision, Barbara Hutton Mdivani von Reventlow had the Regency Room transformed to resemble a street in Casablanca. Eight hundred guests sat down to an all-Moroccan menu at a hundred and seventy tables. Her suite in the hotel was costing her a thousand dollars a day, but when she came through the front door in tennis shorts, Claude barred the way and made her come in the servants' entrance.

He kept records of the whims, desires, dislikes and habits of all clients. Files in his office were consulted with each request for reservations. He looked on it as a duty of his office and took special pride in indulging special wants.

When Ludwig Bemelmans was en route to Paris from Geneva, his pet dog was hit by a car and its back broken. A Swiss veterinarian helped save the animal, but it took days. Bemelmans had to postpone his arrival at the Ritz. He wrote, explaining the reason for the delay. When he came at last— with the dog—he found a soiled and "very un-Ritzlike" blanket on the bed. Beside it was a note from Claude, "Knowing your pet sleeps with you, I procured this cover, which should give you no embarrassment if your friend dirties it."

J. Pierpont Morgan had a favorite suite overlooking the garden. He appeared punctually on the same date every year, and it was always ready for him. But then he arrived on an unexpected visit. Honeymooners were occupying that suite. So Claude offered him other rooms free, and he accepted. "Love ran second to Morgan's money," said Blanche. Claude shrugged.

Claude discovered that whenever a certain German industrialist checked out, his bed was in a different position than when he had checked in. He learned the man always slept with his head to the north, convinced that the motion of the earth affected his brain. Thereafter, when he arrived, the headboard was pointed toward the North Pole, Claude having brought in a compass from his war days to check the direction. The German was easy to please, compared to that early guest, Marcel Proust, who had demanded that his quarters be lined with cork. They were.

"It is necessary that our kind of hotel respond to the wishes of its guests in the best possible manner," said Claude.

But not always.

He made a cautious investigation when laughter, girlish screams and the flapping of wings sounded in the hallway outside a third-floor room. A male guest was watching a trio of naked young ladies trying to catch a covey of doves.

When he told Blanche about the incident, she said dryly, "Perfectly normal behavior. You didn't throw him out, did you?"

"See here, what do you take me for? I told him politely he would have to leave, but first I arranged a reservation for him at the Claridge."

He had a recurring problem with the Brazilian ambassador, whose choice apartment was above the Place Vendôme entrance. It was necessary that the hotel retain access to the rooms in order to hang flags on the staffs that projected from the windowsills. The banners, as the ambassador knew, were to honor prominent foreigners on their arrival. But, the ambassador complained, he hadn't realized when he moved in how many came to the Ritz and how often his apartment had to be invaded. Consequently, he demanded that this inconvenience be curtailed. He sent Claude a list of favored nations whose flags could be flown and asked that others be eliminated.

The memorandum to this effect was delivered to Claude a day before a reigning African sovereign was expected. It seemed an academic problem, as the kingdom was so small that the hotel was unable to locate its flag anyway.

But early next morning a public relations man showed up with one. When Claude refused to display it, the PR man was desolate.

"You will cost me my job," he said.

"You will cost me the lease on a fifty-thousand-dollar-a-year suite," said Claude.

At that moment, the Brazilian strode through the lobby and out of the hotel, bedecked in a splendid morning suit, beribboned and bemedaled. Some important occasion elsewhere obviously required his presence.

"Come quickly," commanded Claude.

They went into the ambassador's apartment and hung the African flag just a few minutes before the potentate drove up, accompanied by a retinue of veiled females, demurely identified on the advance reservation list as domestics. Pleased, the King saluted the banner and then marched into the hotel. Claude hurriedly hauled it in and went below to greet the guest.

A foreign journalist writing a piece about hotel executives once asked Claude, "What does a Managing Directeur do?"

Claude tried to explain, then gave up. "He does all he can do in a normal forty-hour day."

The journalist, comparing the changing scenes of the Ritz to a city, with incidents of birth and death, sickness, suicides, scandals and celebrations, asked if he covered up stories.

"I ask and would like to quote you, Monsieur Auzello. Do you ever suppress headline stories or other newsworthy material?"

"Naturally." He smiled. "But one doesn't talk about them."

The irony, he told Blanche, was that Jean Cocteau, wild with drugs, was making a scene in the lobby at that very moment and had to be ejected. But when he ushered the journalist to the door, the lobby was enjoying its usual normal hush.

Waiting for Claude was a handsome blue-eyed German in his late thirties. He spoke impeccable English, but Blanche preferred to converse with him in German in order to refresh her knowledge of the language. He was happy to oblige.

Baron Hans Gunther von Dincklage was celebrating his recent divorce by practically living in the bar at the Ritz, where he clearly demonstrated his expertise with women, wine, food and cigars, usually in that order. A great table-hopper, he flitted about, making friends, telling the latest jokes, and earning the nickname of Spatz, or Sparrow.

Blanche breezed into Claude's office as "Spatzy" was explaining the reason he was there—"at the request of our mutual friend, Joachim von Ribbentrop. You know, of course, how important he is now in my government, the Third Reich. He has not forgotten the friendliness of the Ritz. . . ."

The Baron went on smoothly, but Blanche could see the frown growing on Claude's face until suddenly he exploded. "Look here! I want no damned bargains of this kind! It is typical of you Nazis to black-market against your own people! I will buy German wines when I need them through proper sources. Go back and tell your boss!"

He jumped up, his face red, and held the door open. Von Dincklage shrugged, kissed Blanche's hand, and left.

Claude returned to his desk. "Germans! They know nothing of subtlety. Do they take me for a fool?"

"Popsy! I've never seen you in such a temper!"

He took a deep breath. "Yes, I should have controlled myself. I must be more discreet."

"What provoked you? Because I like him. He's a real nice guy."

"He is free to move about the hotel where I cannot stop him. But I can stop him from access to the offices and cellars!" He made a note. "I shall give orders."

He looked at her thoughtfully, then said, "Do not think I am suffering from paranoia when I tell you the invasion of France has already begun. This man is a spy!"

9

"I am insulted by the persistent assertion that I want war. Am I a fool? War! It would settle nothing."
—Adolf Hitler in an interview

The delectable life at the Ritz was only peripherally affected by the cruelty and suffering in Spain, where brothers were killing brothers. Old-timers at the hotel viewed the struggle as a minor uprising that would soon be put down. It did seem that way when it began. Marie Louise pointed out that it was not comparable in any way to the war in 1914, when the whole continent was in it.

Victor Rey corroborated that. He had just moved up from receptionist to assistant manager when the hotel closed its doors to the public for eight months. The Germans had reached the Marne River. "The black months," he called them.

There hadn't been enough hospitals to house the wounded, so the Ritz had allowed the medical corps to use the first floor on the Vendôme side as a hospital. When more beds and rooms were needed, the entire Cambon half, too, was given over to the tending of casualties.

Now, in 1937, a small war and a big depression would hardly be enough to close the hotel.

The lobby was a scene of splendid complacency. Only when intellectuals gathered were there unsettling remarks about the combustible state of Europe. Bromfield, ever a cautious fellow, was on hand regularly at Blanche's table. It was his opinion that the action in Spain was a test for a greater fracas to come. He made plans to return to the States, to see to his farm in Ohio and a contract in Hollywood.

In contrast, Hemingway was taking off for the arena itself, to lend a hand to the Loyalists, warning before he departed that men had to take up arms whenever and wherever a clash of ideologies arose.

109

Blanche didn't relate to war horrors. There were no Spanish soldiers in Paris, and the cries of Jews fleeing Nazi Germany weren't heard inside the hotel. Claude could hear the sounds that she did not. He read newspapers every day and listened to radio reports every night. He was concerned and fearful. Said Blanche, "No matter what tomorrow will bring, it worries him today."

"Not for myself," he said. "For you, yes."

One night, after sitting up well past midnight to hear a foreign commentator offer gloomy prognostications, he told an associate, "I shall send Blanche to America and take my chance with that lunatic Boche and his third-rate pack of sex deviates."

"We will not close when this war comes," he promised Marie Louise, who was in agreement. Determined to be ready, he screened the workers on all levels, putting them through psychological interrogations to spot possible defectors. He planned how the silver and linens would be buried in the wine caverns under the hotel. The best vintages, too, of course, would be cemented over. He would leave the less desirable in view, so they would not suspect. Although he said that it was unthinkable that the Nazis could take Paris, he organized the men he trusted into espionage agents. Just in case.

With Bromfield and Hemingway gone, Blanche became aware of changes looming in her life. Even in the best hotels, she said, one only develops transient relationships. In the uncrowded bar, she told Georges Scheuer, who was moving up to replace Frank Meier as head man, "I have a thousand acquaintances and no friends."

Blanche asked Pearl White over for drinks, but getting across Paris caused her extreme pain. She was mixing alcohol and religion, self-prescribing medicines she hoped would cure her ailments. With the help of her parish priest, she built a shrine on her estate at Rambouillet and prayed there daily while swallowing tall brandies. They didn't work, just as her doctor had told her they wouldn't.

She invited Blanche to Rambouillet. What was intended to be a joyous reunion after months of separation turned into an emotional tragedy. Blanche tried to suppress her shock at her friend's appearance, but it showed.

Pearl saw through her forced smile and the murmured "How well you look," and said, "My God, you're still a lousy actress. You're not kidding me. I look like a witch—I know it. A fat witch. Who the hell cares? Come on in and have a drink. The doc says, 'Don't drink any more booze,' but you know me, Blanche. Saying 'Don't!' to me is like saying 'Lights! Camera! Action!' "

Throughout their meeting, Pearl rambled drunkenly on a variety of subjects. "When people ask me why I don't marry Ted, I tell 'em I'm too busy; I'm gonna open a whore house. . . . Got to remember to put you in my will. I don't know whether to leave you Ted or his mother. . . . Whatever became of that Egyptian son-of-a-bitch you were in love with? Still don't know if you were better off marrying that French son-of-a-bitch. . . ."

Suddenly her giggles were erased by a stream of tears. "That poor guy who got killed in my place, remember him? I think of him all the time. It should have been me, it should have been me. And pretty soon I expect to be down there with him so I can tell him."

Two months later she was dead. Blanche attended the funeral on a blistering hot day in August. The priest reminded the gathering of Pearl's greatness in a world that manufactured dreams. But the real and unreal were over, while Blanche sat weeping with memories that no one else in the small chapel could share.

In that depleted period, she felt close to Lily. The little gamin who had accurately forecast what could happen in Spain reacted passionately when the blood and bullets began to fly. She showed up at the hotel, and they went upstairs because Lily wanted a private talk.

She was going to Spain to help fight the Fascists. "For sure, there is something I can do." She was leaving with her compatriot friends, and they were all set to go to the war except for one thing. They had no money.

111

"I should like me if you will give, as loan only, to pay travel expense for me and few others."

It couldn't have come at a worse time. Claude had clamped down again on what he termed Blanche's extraordinary efforts to bankrupt him. He had cut off her allowance and would no longer honor her hotel charges. She took her punishment with equanimity; it was the usual thing between them. It began with the same restrictions; it would be a few weeks and a passionate night before he relented. The current period had just begun. It was out of the question to ask him to help Lily get to Spain.

"I have no money," Blanche said. "If I did, I'd give it to you."

Jewelry? Yes, but pawning or selling would create awkward problems. Some were gifts; she couldn't possibly dispose of those. If she took jewelry to a pawnshop, she would be identified. Claude knew every piece Blanche owned, knew their origins, too—that they came from those neighbors Tiffany, Cartier, Boucheron, Van Cleef and Arpels. If a buyer sought to check their authenticity, it would surely get back to him. He kept records on them with the same precision he kept records of the possessions of the Ritz.

They were in Blanche's rooms on the third floor. It was a hot summer day. Residents of the Rue Cambon were viciously beating dust from their rugs, sounding a thunder like a hundred tom-toms. Hubbub mingled with the cries of street vendors. Blanche went to close the window, and doing so heard a merchant, shoulders draped with rugs and sheepskins, proclaiming that he bought and sold.

There was a fine throw rug on the floor. Blanche sent Lily down to arrange a deal.

The dealer came back the next day, whereupon Blanche leaned from the window and began beating the rug. She let it slip from her grasp, and it was neatly caught by the merchant, who hightailed it around the corner for a rendezvous with Lily, where a satisfactory purchase was effected.

Blanche hurried to Claude's office to berate herself as a butterfingers, a description that was old New Yorkese to her. It made him laugh. She moved herself close to tears over the "accident," and he was touched. He persuaded her to see the absurdity of it. Then he regaled the staff with his account of his "butterfingered baby."

The story even cheered Marie Louise, who was depressed. Victor Rey had died suddenly that week. Though he had long been ill, it came as a special shock to Madame Ritz, severing another tie to César and his memory.

No one ever learned the truth about the rug that fell out the window, reflected Blanche, and the deception seemed worthwhile. "It sure as hell lightened the gloom over Victor Rey."

That was August 1937, and on September 12, an assistant, Zymbruskie, was waiting to felicitate Claude, who was forty-two that day.

"See here, how do you remember my birthday?"

"Easily. It's also my own."

He reached for the phone. "I'm glad you reminded me. I forgot it myself."

Into the phone: "Blanchette, you forgot my birthday. How does such a thing happen?"

"No, I didn't. You're so fussy about growing old I wasn't going to remind you. And besides, I don't have money to buy you a present."

He hung up, smiling.

"She remembered. She is a perfect wife." He sighed and said, "I am obsessed by her. I can only pretend affection for my other woman, but I cannot let go of Blanche."

His feelings were no secret. Gossip about their relationship was an ongoing pastime at the hotel; the personnel relished it with the same passion as the guests.

It was known to all that Claude worshipped the ground Blanche walked on, but it was believed she was "running around," "giving him a hard time." It was said she had many lovers, and a vault filled with diamonds and pearls, gifts of the wealthy international playboys who came in all colors. The heady perfume she affected led to a story that she never bathed, but had a woman come to her twice a week to rub her down with cologne.

Such piquant tales made the gossips watch her with greater

absorption than ever. The yarn about the cologne bath reached Claude, who flew into a rage at the American guest who innocently carried it to him as a conversation piece.

"A base canard!"

Then he reported it to Blanche, who laughed and said, "Of course it's not true. We use perfume!"

As usual, he soon lifted the restrictions against her spending, but meanwhile she took steps to free herself from future penalties. She went into a business partnership with Charlotte Becker, a pleasant little Jewish woman, the only other person besides Lily Kharmayeff whom she felt could be a trusted friend. They opened a workshop in the very center of the important designers on the Avenue George V to cater to the clothes-conscious Paris visitors.

"She was the best dressmaker in Paris, and I was doing people a favor steering them to her. They didn't have to know I was sharing in the profits. But why shouldn't I? Everyone plays that game in Paris."

No scorecard was needed to know the players on the hotel's register in November 1937. More than seventy of its guests that month were among the world's wealthiest and famous. They would, in most cases, retain the sheen of celebrity status, if not their wealth, all their lives. All were names that needed little introduction. A partial list of those staying at the hotel that month included the Duke and Duchess of Kent, Duchess of Sutherland, Earl of Hardwicke, Baron Rudolphe d'Erlanger, Lord Sefton, Lord Astor, Lord Ribbesdale, Lord Queensberry, Sir Alexander and Lady Stewart, Sir Philip Sassoon, His Excellency M. Hore Belisha, Captain and Mrs. Cunningham Reid, Mrs. William Randolph Hearst, Mr. and Mrs. Sumner Wells, General and Mrs. Charles G. Dawes, The Honorable M. Joseph Davies, General J. G. Harbord, Lord and Lady Stanley, Mr. and Mrs. Charles Bedaux, Mr. and Mrs. H. W. Chapin, Mrs. Jimmy Donahue, Mrs. James Corrigan, Countess Wrangel, Count and Countess C. Haugwitz Reventlow, Baron and Baroness von Blixen, Mr. and Mrs. William K. Vanderbilt, and J. Pierpont Morgan.

By summer of 1938, the astute observers realized that Spain's civil war between its liberals and fascistic government forces was just a preliminary bout, with the main event still ahead on the program. War clouds drifting over from Germany threatened all Europe. Finally, France mobilized more than two million men. It was inevitable that Claude would be called up in a larger conflict because of his reserve officer status.

Meanwhile he had time to look to the manner in which the hotel could function if he wasn't around. He set up a chain of command and plotted logistics as though the enemy had already taken Place Vendôme. Blanche said he showed a kind of delight in working out strategies. After all, he had not studied the life of Napoleon for nothing.

When wars approach, he observed, half the world believes itself obligated to sit still and wait, and the other half dances.

"We have decided against self-restraint; we shall continue to conserve the traditions of the Ritz while doing our part to maintain the prestige and magic of Paris," quoted the society magazine *L'Elite de Paris* in an article that took note of his World War I record as an artillery officer decorated with the Croix de Guerre and the Légion d'Honneur.

The piece went on in flowery language to report, "He is strongly qualified to speak about the elegant life in Paris. For a long time he has possessed an extensive acquaintance with a clientele counted among the most select in the entire world."

Thereupon, he inaugurated a series of Sunday night dinner-dances, a first for the Ritz and all hotels in Paris, borrowed from a popular custom in America and a growing vogue in London. But although the sophisticated lilt of Maestro Leo Reisman's orchestra lured the social leaders of the city, Americans were disappearing from view. Those who remained were comforted by word that the embassy was prepared to handle their evacuation, if and when needed.

Journalists settled around Blanche's table in the bar, a restless, hard-drinking lot, spreading old rumors and bringing in new, as they raced in and out of Paris, in and out of London,

115

in and out of Berlin. Vincent Sheean, William L. Shirer, A. J. Liebling, H. R. Knickerbocker and John Gunther became regulars in the bar.

Formeedarb was how Blanche described Dorothy Thompson, a stalwart with a byline growing in popularity around the world—everywhere, that is, except Germany, where she and her writings were banned. More of an observer than a reporter, she stood up to Hitler personally and warned everyone to be skeptical of his promises.

Forceful and colorful but pessimistic, she had a dynamism and charisma that shot her into the forefront of the new breed. After arriving in Paris as the wife of the celebrated novelist Sinclair Lewis, she was reversing the positions—he was being called the husband of Dorothy Thompson. She fascinated all who congregated at Blanche's table with her discourses on current events.

But Blanche gauged the political turmoil of Europe by the guest list of the hotel. When crises heightened, there were more empty rooms and less business for Mrs. Becker, two consequences that mattered very much.

"Dorothy Thompson's my kind of woman," Blanche said. "But I wish she'd stop saying Europe is doomed. She's frightening away our customers."

In October, Premier Daladier and Prime Minister Chamberlain returned from meeting Hitler in Munich. The Britisher announced, "Peace in our time," while the French leader, having served as Minister of Defense, was less sanguine. He echoed the sentiments expressed by Chamberlain, but added, "We have reached the limit of our concessions."

An optimistic society invaded the Ritz again. Ballroom reservations were stacked up in Claude's office. Gaiety that had faded from sight in the political fog emerged into the clear. Festivities erupted nightly, well organized and very lavish, parties paid for by the international rich, some arranged by at least one of the international poor.

Elsa Maxwell was the big noise at party-throwing. A plump egotist, she was expert at the game. "Pudgy and pushy" was how Blanche described her. It was a case of dislike at first sight.

Elsa had a knack for finding overprivileged Americans who thought their social status underprivileged. For a fee, she transformed un-notables into notables, using the publicity surrounding their galas to the best possible advantage for them and herself. She preferred to give her soirees at the Ritz, and because of the money she brought in, Claude allowed her rare favors. He provided a room "on the cuff" so she could use the hotel as her address to enhance her standing with prospective clients.

Janet Flanner, who covered the Paris scene in books and for the *New Yorker* magazine, wrote avidly of the goings-on at the Maxwell masquerades and fancy-dress parties. Describing one of these, she reported, "Chanel did a land-office business generally, cutting and fitting gowns for the young men about town who appeared as some of the best-known women in Paris." For another, in which the invited were asked to wear something white, "the most acclaimed entree was made in fabulous white-plaster masks and wigs concocted by Jean Cocteau and Christian Berard."

In her book *American in Paris,* Flanner reported, "At an enormous gala at the Ritz, Elsa Maxwell ordered the man who was paying for it to leave because he was so drunk."

Blanche scoffed. "Elsa? Never! Not if he was footing the bill."

She also ridiculed a widely circulated story that millionaire Ralph Beaver Strassburger offered Elsa $5,000 and let her choose whether to use it to buy a Cartier jewel for herself or to pay to have Fritz Kreisler play at a party Strassburger was giving at the Ritz. It was reported Elsa chose Kreisler.

Blanche called it "pure sham. Elsa loved money and jewelry a damn sight more than hearing a fiddle!"

But the story gained worldwide publicity, and when George Bernard Shaw heard it he pronounced Elsa Maxwell the eighth wonder of the world and asked to meet her.

"L'affaire Maxwell," as Blanche called Claude's fascination

with the lady, ended when Elsa ignored a large bill for drinks. To collect it, Claude dispatched Georges Scheuer to the flat where the party-giver lived on the Left Bank, at 2, Rue Git-le-Coeur. She greeted the young barman at the door, heard the reason for his coming, then crossed to a full-length bureau. When she opened the top drawer, Georges reported, "It was so full of francs, they spilled out and fell all over the floor."

The sight of this cash seemed to mesmerize Elsa. She slammed the drawer shut, took a few centimes from her purse, and held them out.

"This is for you, my man," she said. "Tell Monsieur Auzello I'll come by and settle his bill when I can find time."

Then, like many of the party-throwers, she left for America. The "Peace in Our Time" was crumbling, and Europe continued to empty out, as those who could afford it took off, like bystanders at a spectacle jumping off a shaky grandstand.

The Spanish civil war ended in the spring of 1939. More than a quarter of a million Loyalist sympathizers crossed into France, which accepted them reluctantly and held them as prisoners of peace in barbed-wire enclosures. Released slowly, some of these vanquished filtered into Paris. Blanche went to the building where Lily lived, to see if she was back. But the grubby *propriétaire* had no information at all, and a new tenant in the room wouldn't even open the door.

Claude was devoting spare hours to studying prewar's historical meanings and what they might foretell. But realities moved faster than he could theorize. In June Hitler announced that he wanted to repossess the Polish-owned Danzig corridor that connected the Baltic Sea to East Prussia because it had been German territory during the twelfth century and again in the eighteenth. The region was known as the powder keg of Europe. Kicking it back and forth was like using a bomb for a football.

As a consequence, the events of early summer provided Paris with a day-to-day climate of suspense. Young soldiers filled trains that took them north to the German frontier, and foreign civilians crowded those that took them west to the sea.

Children were moved to the country. Stay-at-homes stood on the boulevards and read posters that told them how to live in blackouts and behave in a bombing attack and try to survive gas and, for the good of all, avoid hoarding food.

When the exodus had slowed and the posters no longer attracted, August arrived idyllic and peaceful. Dim blue lights supplied nocturnal illumination on streets that always scintillated so exquisitely after dark. The din and crush of traffic disappeared, and so did customers in the Ritz. There were few reservations for September, but nothing that Claude could do about it. The nations of the world held their collective breath.

From Hollywood, Herman wrote Blanche to come to California, where he was employed in the music department at Warner Brothers Studio, adding lyrical flourishes to a production line of movies that sang of escapism—escape from truth and reality.

He enclosed a photo of himself, smiling but haggard and flabby. Yes, he wrote her, he still used that stuff, but it was a medical necessity. He was registered, and the law allowed him to get it by prescription.

Claude urged her to go and stay awhile in the sunshine. He was terribly worried for her, fearful she couldn't cope in a world without him.

J'Ali wrote her to get out of France and come to him. In familiar rhetorical style, he described how the warm Egyptian sun would heat her heart into a glowing coal of desire. She didn't mention it to Claude, telling herself the evasion wasn't to avoid his displeasure—she could handle that—but because things J'Ali had once said still lurked in her mind and made it probable he was pro-German. She was not prepared to handle that.

The American ambassador was seen almost daily in the Ritz. William C. Bullitt loved the social spotlight. He and Blanche met often. He had been an executive in a film company in New York during the 1920s, and they discovered a common interest in movies. He labeled himself an author for having written a novel, *It's Not Done,* and claimed to be related to Fletcher Christian, leader of the mutiny that occurred on

119

H.M.S. *Bounty*. The C that Bullitt always wrote in his signature stood for Christian, and the film picturization was a long-running hit on the Champs-Elysées. He made a point of that when he was in the company of actors and actresses.

Blanche wasn't fond of him; it was an instinctive feeling, and it embarrassed her because of his position as the American representative. Claude knew much more about him than she did, because of his way of delving into personalities. It was no secret that Bullitt was a favorite of President Franklin D. Roosevelt, and it was also known that as ambassador to Russia he had subjected the White House to a barrage of cables about happenings in the Kremlin so ludicrous that Roosevelt had no choice but to post him elsewhere. He transferred him to France, which accepted him with characteristic nonchalance. Blanche didn't know or care about that, but she had her own opinion of the ambassador: "If he isn't a fairy, he gives a good imitation of one." With so many functions in the hotel for him to attend, she saw him often but never by choice.

However, there was little traffic in the lobby the day in late August when he confronted her. In fact, she immediately suspected he had been looking for her.

"When will you be going home, Madame Auzello?"

"I have no plans."

"I'm advising all Americans to leave. It is imperative. I cabled the President that war is inevitable."

"I've never seen a war. Would you believe it?"

"Really, it's no time for levity. You can believe me!"

"Oh, I do!"

"Your husband and I have been discussing the situation."

"Ahhhh, I see."

"He did not speak of you. It was about the hotel, actually. He understands the seriousness we face. In regard to the hotel, I mean. I don't suppose he tells you; no man likes to frighten his wife."

"I don't frighten easily. I guess he knows that by now."

He stepped back pettishly. "I can't order you to leave, but I most certainly advise it." He turned and walked away.

120

It was late that night before Claude asked if she had happened to see the ambassador.

"You silly bastard," she said. "I knew the minute he started to talk that it was a put-up job. I bet you told him what to say. Stop trying to get rid of me."

The climactic hour struck at the end of August. In spite of all the tense moments that preceded it, it was sudden and with an unexpected twist. Stalin's Russia and Hitler's Germany signed a non-aggression pact. Negotiated in secrecy, it was all the dictators needed. Hitler turned his legions loose on Poland. Flotillas of Stuka dive-bombers turned bricks and flesh into masses of red rubble.

Blanche was in the somber group assembled in Claude's office to listen to the radio and await the inevitable announcement. Finally it came, in a broadcast with Daladier of France and Chamberlain of England echoing each other: "This country is at war with Germany."

"Look here," Claude told them, "we have just heard the most important words we will ever hear in our lifetime."

At that moment, the Cambon concierge rapped on the door and came in, saw the group and hesitated.

"Well, what is it?" asked Claude.

"A young sailor is here with a girl. They are newlyweds and find our rates too high. It is their dream, they say, to spend their first night at the Ritz. Perhaps, Monsieur Auzello, in view of—you would be willing . . ."

"Give them a bridal suite," he commanded. "And sandwiches and champagne. And send a bottle here to us."

Then: "Look here, how marriages increase when wars begin. Let us advertise special rates for those just married. That should fill some empty rooms."

The champagne arrived and they drank. The idea of soliciting newlyweds excited them, and there were jokes. Claude clinked his glass with hers and said, "Blanchette, there is still time for you to go home."

She shook her head. "I am home."

10

"It is because of luxury and the vanity of women that great empires crumble."
—Benjamin Franklin

"I don't know why I stayed. There was no emotion involved or special feelings. It didn't seem a heroic thing to do; maybe it was the rebel in me—maybe I wanted to stay because everyone was telling me to go.

"Of course, I loved Claude and Paris and the Ritz, and I was damned if I'd let the Germans come between us.

"In the back of my mind, there may have been other reasons—that trip to New York, when I saw it had become my second home instead of my first. So why go back?

"And Pearl. Her spirit, anyway. The Germans couldn't have chased her away; you could bet your life on that. She was always playing Pauline, no matter what other name they gave her. One of her films was called *Pearl of the Army;* it was romantic and exciting and fun. That was before she got crippled. She was young and beautiful then, and I thought to myself, That's how I am now. In Egypt she was so gloomy, irritable, complaining. It was awful. I told myself that if I ran away back to the States, it would be sure proof I'd grown old.

"Those are the reasons, I guess, why I stayed. Anyway, I never once considered leaving."

Claude's orders were to report immediately to the garrison at Nîmes, in Provence.

"I'm going with you," she said.

"Are you crazy? You will stay here."

"You haven't put on your uniform yet, and you're a general!"

"See here, I am your husband. I outrank a general!"

He saw a look in her eye, the psychic knowledge that devel-

123

ops between those who have shared sufficient beds and lives and loves. He could divine what she was thinking.

"No. She will not be there either."

"How do I know?"

"Madame, you are intolerable. You know because I tell you. Besides, we are practically finished."

"Because of the war?"

"Because of you."

"I've never seen her."

"You have, but didn't know. Anyway, she has decided. I agree with her. I shall be occupied with other matters."

"You can find another after the war."

"Probably." He smiled.

She smiled, too. "I'll help you look."

They made a sentimental tour of the hotel, walking hand in hand.

Everyone assured everyone that their army would soon take care of Hitler. An old janitor predicted the world would soon be back to normal. Claude the philosopher said, "Ah, but look here, Antoine, fighting is normal, peace is abnormal." And Claude the historian added, "Since the world began, there is always fighting somewhere."

All males of military age were leaving, and Marie Louise was taking charge. Claude saved his last farewell for her.

"Don't go yet," she said, and sent for tea.

"I never felt as close to Madame Ritz as I did that day," Blanche said. "I knew then how much she valued Claude. She kept praising him, talking about her husband and others at the hotel in the past and how he stood right up there beside them. I guess he liked it; he sat through a lot of stories he must have known as well as she did."

They exchanged anecdotes about Victor Rey, a favorite of both.

"There was that time his wife was having a baby," she said. "Poor Victor, he was stuck at Reception when the word came that she was in labor. An Englishman, very big, very important, offered to take over so he could go to the hospital."

"Victor liked to tell that story," said Claude. "The man was Lord Northcliffe."

"Yes, it was before they knighted him. I think he deserved it just for that. You know, Blanche, that while he was behind the desk he showed a large suite to a party of Americans who took it and didn't know until the next day that he wasn't the regular clerk. Then Victor Rey said to this famous Englishman, 'Why don't we exchange jobs?'"

They spoke of their famous chef de cuisine, Auguste Escoffier, César's friend and acknowledged king of French culinary arts. After Escoffier left to preside over the kitchens of the Carlton and the Ritz in London, he only conversed in French. "I was afraid that if I learned their language I might learn their way of cooking, too."

He was a gallant, chivalrous fellow who named each new creation for singers and actresses of his acquaintance. His menus listed Salade Rejane, Coupe Melba and Toast Melba, Poires Mary Garden, Coupe Yvette, Consommé Bernhardt, Poularde Adelina Patti. Crêpes Suzette, one of his most lasting triumphs, was never identified. Suzette was believed to be one of Edward VII's roommates at the Ritz, but Escoffier refused to confirm it.

Marie Louise thought that Escoffier's successor, Chef Olivier, was the kindliest man who had worked for her. Another thoughtful fellow, a guest during the 1914 world war, was Marcel Proust. Olivier and Proust were the best of friends. Yes, Proust could be demanding, but it was offset by his solicitude for others. And there was Proust's friend, Colette, who was often with him when she, too, stayed in the hotel.

"A wonderful way with words, the two of them," said Marie Louise. "She, that sparkling young woman, and he, old but delicate, speaking always with expressive gestures, standing outside under the colonnade for what may have been hours in the night, talking, talking—as I am talking now."

Then Claude said he had to go. Marie Louise embraced him and said, "My happiest moment will be when you come back to us."

As an officer he could live off the post in Nîmes. He took advantage of that and moved into a flat in the ancient city. The war was oddly dormant; the expected German blitzkrieg hadn't materialized.

Two weeks after he arrived, he unlocked the door and found Blanche unpacking her bags. She had talked the concierge into letting her in.

He sat down, slapped his knees hard with exasperation, and asked, "Why are you here?"

"Because I want to be with you. Because Paris is dull without you. Because I want to be a good French wife."

"About time," he growled.

She promised to get rid of all her mannerisms that rubbed him the wrong way. She meant it, too.

"From now on, you're the boss." That prerogative, as she knew, was every Frenchman's cherished hope and privilege.

"Then, see here, you will do nothing without telling me."

"Yes." Another promise, meant to be kept. "All French wives mean to keep the promises they make their husbands," she reflected. "I had good intentions, too."

In a few days, she was bored.

"What a war! Are they all like this?"

The war, indeed, was no war at all. When the Germans failed to attack, the French relaxed in and behind the Maginot Line.

Nîmes was a center for wine- and brandy-making. It was almost as cheap to bathe in vin rouge as to drink the water. That, she noted, was an advantage if one had to sit out *La Drôle de Guerre* or "The Phony War."

Claude enlivened his hours in arguments with fellow officers that they disguised as debates. In essence, they were friendly differences of opinion that started in the barracks and continued after dark in the Auzello apartment.

Blanche was often called upon to referee. It came as a surprise to many that she would never allow her judgment to be influenced by Claude's point of view. Once, when she decreed his opponent the winner, he said, "Western civilization has been set back a hundred years because America educated

Blanche to think." But he said it softly, smiling, and with a loving look at her.

To help her pass the burdensome hours of small-town existence, he brought her books about Nîmes, which he pored through himself with great relish. For her special attention he underlined a passage by Colette, who had visited there with a touring group of players.

She described its gardens of La Fontaine:

So fairylike that one trembles lest it dissolve in a mist: the shimmering water of Diane's Bath, green, dark, transparent, brilliant as a serpent, trees with mauve blossoms, a shower of perfumed rain that rolls in heavy pearls, warm to the taste like jonquils. One wants to lie down in Nimes with a sigh, to sleep and never wake up.

Blanche sallied into the described places, dutifully trudged through the walled city, its ancient sites, the amphitheater, temples and Roman baths.

She soon gave up.

"I'm not in tune with small towns. I don't relate to people who live in them. I see why Colette just wanted to sleep and never wake up. There's nothing else to do."

Hugo Becker, the son of her erstwhile dressmaker partner, had applied for service in the artillery and hoped to be inducted into Claude's regiment.

He filled out the necessary papers, and Claude undertook to arrange it.

"It won't be easy," he told Blanche.

"Why?"

He shrugged evasively. "It never is."

Then, discarding his usual direct approach, he scanned her passport and said casually, "Ah, yes. I think now it was wise to change your religion."

"Why do you worry about that? I never think of it."

He had reason to worry. The virus of anti-Semitism was spreading into France; its contagion was obvious, on the field and in the barracks. It was very visible to him in the person of his immediate superior.

127

Colonel Deschamps tried unsuccessfully to block young Becker's transfer; Claude won out because the youth's record showed him to be an excellent gunner. The only reasons advanced against him were unmistakably racist.

But if actual proof was needed, Claude got it from one of the debate group who stayed on after the others had left. "Our Colonel warned me to look out, you're a Jew-lover. I thought you ought to know. He doesn't like Blanche, either. Says she acts like she's too good for army life."

Claude smiled. "She is."

He warned her to keep her opinions to herself, especially when she moved among the townspeople.

"There are German sympathizers about, and you have no way of knowing who they are."

"Germans don't frighten me."

"Me neither, Blanchette. But you do."

Because the United States was neutral, he felt that her American citizenship was her best protection. Every morning he reminded her to carry her passport.

He was relieved that the arrival of Hugo Becker sparked a project that could keep her busy. She offered to help get his sister and parents out of Paris and find a place for them in the country.

A boy who worked in the baker's shop, still too young for the army but old enough to operate the ancient smoking Panhard rented from their landlord, drove her around the countryside. Because the declared war was in limbo, uncertainty was in the air—city people moving out of the cities, farm folk moving out of farms.

"They expect the merry-go-round will take them somewhere safe, forgetting that it always brings you back to where you were," observed Claude of these migrations.

The rural neighborhood, tranquil and serene, owed its idyllic reputation to the illustrated dreams of great artists. The farmhouse she selected for the Beckers gave indications of being an ideal hideout, isolated a half-mile from a sleepy village, a quarter of a mile from a running stream, and millions of miles from the turmoil of civilization.

Claude congratulated her on the acquisition, and Charlotte Becker and her husband Marcel were enchanted. Neighboring peasant-farmers, their acres scattered across the landscape, raised their own vegetables and pigs and fowl, and each owned a single milk cow. The Beckers planned to do the same; it would help them melt into the background. They also planned to assume the same uncommunicative attitude as their neighbors. It was a time to remain apart from strangers.

Behind blackout shades, Claude and Marcel Becker passed an entire winter in enjoyable arguments over the pros and cons of the nation's rulers, notably young Reynaud and old Pétain. Were they able, honest or corrupt; were they dilettante or professional, too indulgent or too despotic? There were arguments, too, over whether France should attack the monster in Berlin or negotiate. Many of Claude's fellow officers believed Stalin a greater enemy than Hitler. There were no decisions reached, but it was a way to pass a war that was no war.

Claude was loving the serenity of Provence as much as Blanche disliked it.

"See here, why not stay on the farm with Marcel and Charlotte? In a short time, we will take the offensive. My regiment is ready to move as soon as we get the word."

"The day you move out of here, I'm heading back to Paris."

"What's that? No! I forbid you! You will stay on the farm or in Nîmes. The Boche won't waste his bombs here, I can tell you, and I won't need to worry about you."

When it happened, there was small consolation that he had been right about Nîmes. There were no bombs.

The blitzkrieg roared in after months of tense inactivity; Italy joined the Nazi side for little reason except that Mussolini thought Hitler a winner. The Luftwaffe overflew, and the tanks bypassed the Maginot Line through the low countries. Most French commanders quit cold, but some shot themselves and others shot the men who ran away. Reynaud wanted to fight on, and Pétain wanted to capitulate. For two days and nights nobody knew what was happening, including Blanche and Claude and everyone assembled in the garrison at Nîmes. It was a forgotten post, with men and guns ready but no enemy to use them against. There were no orders of any kind.

During that first week in June 1940, there was total confusion at the Ritz. People ran in and out with the latest rumors. The Germans were at the gates of the city, the Germans had been turned back, Paris was being declared an open city and the German bombers were on their way, everyone should leave at once, but wait, because the roads were cluttered with wheeled vehicles, from bicycles to pushcarts to motorbikes to horse-drawn wagons to baby carriages to late model automobiles. At night one heard footsteps running through the Place Vendôme and sometimes a woman's frantic scream, but the march of German boots that one expected to hear didn't materialize until the second week. Then radios that had been tuned to empty air suddenly came alive; a broadcast from Bordeaux reported France was asking for a truce. The splendor that was France was finished, lost, and the great days of elegance in the hotel were gone, too. The staff shed tears for both.

Hitler controlled 3000 miles of Europe, from Norway's North Cape to the Spanish Pyrenees. Even those not weeping didn't sleep. The surrender was broadcast at 12:35 A.M.

The order was posted at the garrison at Nîmes. Each captain was to handle his regiment's paperwork, take back the military equipment, and make his men civilians again and send them home. It was to be done quickly and without ceremony.

But Claude assembled his regiment on the parade ground and said his own goodbye:

Gunners—my friends! As soon as I heard the news of this abominable armistice I thought I must see you immediately because I felt you must be heartbroken.

I want you to know that nothing is lost. France has seen more tragic moments and has always risen again.

The war is only beginning. The Germans are not yet the victors.

Our ally, England, thanks to her situation, will resist for a long time—and victoriously. Other nations will join her, and we ourselves will return to the battle.

When you get back to your firesides, work. Work hard and keep in your hearts hope and unshaken confidence in our beloved France.

He drew cheers from his men but a sharp denunciation from Colonel Deschamps. "When you are conquered, you bow. We are conquered!"

"Speak for yourself," snapped Claude.

He wrote out his own certificate of demobilization and signed it. He also wrote the pass he needed for himself and Blanche to enter Paris.

They took the train, a sad journey in a car of silent passengers, dispirited and devastated, trying to cope with a future curtained off by a state of affairs no one had foreseen and they still couldn't believe.

The city was already occupied and governed by the victors. Claude engaged two young boys to carry their luggage to the Place Vendôme. When they had the hotel in sight, one boy ran away because he saw armed sentries at the entrance.

Only officers of the German army were being allowed through the *porte-cochère*.

"Come, we'll go to the Avenue Montaigne," Claude told Blanche.

"Don't be so nervous," she told him.

She gazed stonily at the sentry barring their way. "You! Get an officer out here!" she commanded in German. *"Mach schnell!"*

He saluted and went inside, and she winked at Claude. "You see how I handle them?"

The sentry returned with a Lieutenant-Colonel who politely explained that the management of the hotel had been relocated on the Cambon side.

"Then have your men carry our bags for us," she said.

Two German soldiers, laden down with all their luggage, circled the hotel. They followed, arm in arm, Claude amazed, Blanche complacent.

131

Neither knew that a message had come from Berlin, part of the new science called Psychological Warfare:

Our Führer decrees we must extend courtesy and help and friendship and not antagonize the defeated people of France.

11

"You didn't hear cannons in the Ritz, but the war was fought there, too."
—Claude Auzello

"It worked for you this time, but when it fails you will see how they behave!"

Then, as he was telling her to pattern herself after him, she looked up from the unpacking.

"Claude Auzello, you are a fraud!"

Blank demobilization papers and French passport stamps were stuffed in a compartment.

"I see why you didn't want to go in the front door. Suppose they searched us? You didn't even tell me. Your wife!"

Then she laughed at the comic aspects—German soldiers carrying his stolen documents into the hotel—and when he saw the point he laughed louder than she did.

He commanded her to sit down and listen to him. He was pointing his finger in all directions and shaking it as he spoke—it was tied to his new habit of valuing the words he was about to say and putting them in order the way he itemized material things. This would be "the most important talk of our lives. You will remember everything I tell you.

"Look here, a man in uniform has a permit to kill. When I was in uniform I had the permit. Now the Boche wears the uniform. You see the difference?

"You are no longer a child. You must give up your capricious actions, the kind you love to indulge in. I believe with all my heart that France will triumph in the end, but this day, today, is a sweet moment to be German. And they are not a gracious people. You will see how they rape and pillage. I know. It is man's nature to piss on his enemies and flagellate and destroy."

"Yes, Popsy"

"It started with the caveman; he went after the women. What exultation! To strip them, beat them, force them into fornication in manners I will not even try to describe! Then—they turn on them, kill them in horrifying ways. I know; I tell you because even we French, yes, I regret, we, too—I cannot say we are saints. If the German is different, it is only that he is the most cold-hearted animal on earth. But only in that degree is he different!"

She kept nodding her head and finally said, "Yes, Popsy, I understand. I will be careful." But to herself, she claimed, she was thinking, "I'm amazed. He really doesn't know me as well as I thought he did. How can he believe that I'm going to be in the center of a war and do nothing?"

On the other side of the coin, Claude knew even then that the Ritz would make a marvelous observation post against the enemy, far more comfortable but otherwise not too dissimilar from the box he had occupied near the woods during the first world war.

"The situation is heartbreaking," declared Marie Louise Ritz. The hotel, like France under the armistice terms, was divided into two zones. Just as the quasi-French government was set up in the south, the hotel management was set up on the Cambon side. On the Vendôme side, across the line of demarcation, the Germans had taken over. But their commands had to be obeyed all through the hotel, exactly as they had to be all through France.

When their armies were approaching Paris, a report that the Ritz would close reached Georges Mandel, Minister of the Interior, who wanted to preserve all aspects of normality in the city. He informed Marie Louise that the government was trying to effect an armistice. The fall of France was a certainty. Meanwhile, Paris was declared an open city.

If she closed the hotel, he said, it would be requisitioned by and staffed by Nazis. "Then you will never get it back, Madame Ritz."

That decided her. There were less than twenty workers still on duty. She switched elevator operators to the concierge desks and chasseurs to the elevators, then handled a stint on the telephone switchboard herself. While they were reorganizing, the electric system went dead, the phones, lights, elevators stopped, and she and everyone else just waited.

"We waited for what? Bombs? Cannons? The Germans were at the gates. For two days and nights our hotel was isolated. No one went out; we were like a desert island. Think of that, in the center of Paris.

"Then came the sounds of those awful brass bands, nothing like our beautiful music, and they were marching into the Place de la Concorde. We heard them singing; they were so happy, not at all like the business-minded, humorless people who came to the hotel.

"The electricity came on, and Generals Halder and Bock drove up and asked for breakfast. You can imagine how heavy our hearts were. After they left, I went for a walk and saw a big red flag with a swastika flying from the Crillon and another on the Eiffel Tower!"

It took forty-eight hours for the Germans to secure Paris in their best interests. Their surprisingly affable display of manners disarmed the Parisians to such an extent that almost all its patriotic rebels accepted the restrictions imposed on them, and when Blanche and Claude arrived the atmosphere was relaxed, the Cambon side was doing business as usual.

The officer who had assigned the soldiers to carry their bags appeared at their rooms the next morning even before Claude had settled into the job of running the hotel again. He carried a locked briefcase. He was the standard Teutonic type, a close-cropped haircut, peach-clean complexion, immaculate uniform. His self-assurance bordered on the abrasive.

"Perfect casting," said Blanche.

"Colonel Ebert," he announced and tossed off a stiff salute. "Erich Ebert."

Blanche removed dresses and lingerie from a chair slowly, taking her time to decide where to put them in the disheveled room, and the opportunity to cast an inquisitive look at Claude. Meanwhile the Colonel unlocked a sheaf of papers, set them on a table, pulled the chair close, and sat down. He was exuding affability.

He offered gold-tipped cigarettes from a monogrammed case. Claude waved them off politely. Blanche popped one of her Gauloises in her mouth, and as the German proffered his lighter she produced a match box and lit it for herself. Then she blew a long puff of smoke into the air, quite aware that the aroma could be offensive. But Nîmes had taught her to like strong French cigarettes.

"I was resolved from the beginning, no matter what Claude said, to make every German know how I felt toward him."

The Colonel spoke English with a deep, cultured voice. "I envy you your languages, Captain Auzello," he said, tapping the papers to indicate the source of his information. "I speak good German, fair English and some Chinese. I am ashamed that I know nothing of the Latin languages."

He launched into a description of China, where he had spent five years. He had returned on holiday to Hamburg, he told them, to see his parents just when Hitler was demanding the return of Danzig. "To which he was entitled. I saw how my country was threatened by England and Poland and I stayed, although I did not foresee war."

"But look here, surely you were in the army then," said Claude.

The Colonel gave him a shrewd appraisal. He picked up the papers and without looking through them told Claude it was a dossier of his hotel and army background and how he had handled the situation the day of the general strike.

Claude fidgeted through the recital, fearful of what their visitor knew about Blanche.

"You make an excellent choice as manager, Monsieur Auzello. So, we are pleased to have you continue. At least for the present. We shall soon have General von Stulpnagel staying in the hotel; maybe he will make changes, but meanwhile you will contact me for what is needed."

Returning the papers to his case, he stopped, scanned a page, then held it up. One word was scrawled across it: ENJUIVE.

"We know you French are hospitable, but we shall not allow Jews to betray your hospitality any longer." To Blanche: "You are American-born, are you not, Madame Auzello?"

She nodded.

"A magnificent country. I saw it for the first time on my way home. I was on the train from Chicago the night of the Fourth of July. You celebrate your independence from England, yes? I watched through the window for a display of fireworks. But there was a rain, and I saw nothing."

"It happens."

"You know that part of the country?"

"What part?"

"I was traveling between Chicago and New York."

"Naturally."

"Ah, yes, you were born . . ."

"In Ohio. If it was a clear night you would have seen the house where I was born. The tracks ran quite near." She gave him her only smile. "But my family moved away when I was three."

After he had gone, she said to Claude, "My God, you turned white when he started on me."

"What luck that you knew the answers."

"You needn't worry. I'll always take care of myself."

He could congratulate himself, too, because he had perceived that the Colonel was in China with the army. A Chinese importer who often stayed in the hotel had told him there were German military advisers there. Thoughtfully, he reviewed all the implications of Colonel Ebert's visit and warned Blanche not to be taken in by anything he had said, including his avowal of his linguistic limitations.

"Look here, I wager he speaks French very well. You see how you must be careful! We've had luck with this fellow. I hope it doesn't run out."

"Oh, you!" she said. "Always worrying."

Reminiscence time. . . .

"When I lived in New York, I'd run into kids I knew who were going into a new play. They'd carry around a wrinkled bunch of typed pages like they were leaves of gold. Their sides, they called them, the cues and lines they were supposed to learn. They'd chew my ear off telling me how they got called to a reading with the director, who gave them his interpretation—how their character figured in the plot, how they must look, how they should walk and talk and listen, and even what they should be thinking. I wanted to act on Broadway, too, but I never got that far. It was a rough game. I got brutal turndowns, runarounds and brush-offs. You come up against tough, ugly little agents and guys who've got something different on their minds than you do. It was that way around the movie studios, too, but I sort of laughed those guys out of it, and anyway, movie jobs were easier to find.

"I kept remembering those days all the time Claude was telling me how I was to act in the days ahead. I didn't want to fool him, God knows, but I thought, at last I can show the world I'm a damn good actress. Well, I must have been looking into a private crystal ball, because I didn't play one part, I played three, and I bet if I'd had an audience when I did my big scenes I'd have brought the house down! Sarah Bernhardt couldn't have done them better!"

General Otto von Stulpnagel and Hans Speidel took suites at the Ritz with the air of pleasant anticipation that was typical of guests who had checked in in happier days. Nazi officers and officials were moving into all the first-class Paris hotels to see that their directives were obeyed.

Field Marshal Gerd von Rundstedt, who led the German First Army in the breakthrough of France all the way to Dunkirk, was at the George V; Ambassador to Paris Otto Abetz was at the Hôtel Iéna; another ambassador, Franz von Papen, famed for combining espionage with diplomacy, was at the Lancaster. Others billeted themselves at the Claridge, Bristol and Meurice. The main German communications center was set up in the Majestic.

Not all of Hitler's men were as well disposed to the French as the pair who settled into the Ritz; but, like them, they all enjoyed the pleasures that Paris afforded them. The ugly abbreviation *collabo* was yet unheard.

Postal and telephone service had been restored. Ration cards had been distributed. The new rulers of the city advised the top entertainers it would be helpful to go right on entertaining. The big cabaret at the Casino de Paris was back in action starring Maurice Chevalier and Josephine Baker.

Along with Charles Trenet, they sang the glories of *La Vie Parisienne,* while Edith Piaf mourned of lost love in gay Paree. Patriots were horrified. Claude told Blanche, "We will not patronize any of the amusements," in a tone of voice that clearly indicated he would hear no arguments.

Audiences were small, although curfew was only lightly enforced, as the Nazis hoped to win the citizenry into a friendly alliance. The controlled radio broadcasts mixed propaganda with reminders that Sascha Guitry could be seen in a repertory of sexy comedies. Also, *Cyrano de Bergerac* and *Madame Sans-Gêne,* native classics based on love, one the male and one the female point of view, could be enjoyed at the Comédie Française.

There was no artificially stimulated fun at the Ritz, but authentic joy showed when favorite employees straggled in. Georges Scheuer returned from his disordered regiment without discharge papers, so Claude signed and gave him one he had brought from Nîmes, and kept beneath the floor of his new office on the Cambon side, covered by a rug and a desk.

There were whispers that the Germans, for all their benevolent exteriors, were dealing harshly with transgressors. Workers told him they knew people who were arrested, imprisoned, deported. But those arrests, when they occurred, were subtly handled. None was authenticated, but each had enough substance to warrant caution.

At the command of Colonel Ebert, Claude appeared in the suite taken over by the newly arrived General Otto von Stulpnagel. The officer, relaxed and informal, said how much he admired the hotel and the way it made its guests comfortable. He had only the highest regard for its conveniences and cuisine. He would get a personal sampling next evening, when a banquet was being given in his honor.

Claude agreed to see to it that all went well. Outside the suite, he reminded Colonel Ebert that ration cards were required.

"Surely not for an officer of Stulpnagel's stature!" said Ebert.

The next evening the tables contained all the requisites of a sumptuous banquet except food.

While waiters stood by, empty-handed, Claude walked in and reminded the guests that their own directive about rationing explicitly included members of the German army. There was a howl of laughter, but Claude stood his ground. The meal was delayed, but the Germans took it good-naturedly, downing unrationed wine and beer until sufficient permits could be rounded up.

Next morning, Claude was again summoned to the General. He was as friendly as ever.

"I see your problem, Monsieur Auzello. You were quite right to do what you did. But hereafter, we shall supply our food from our own warehouses. That way, we won't require ration cards."

However, as the the hotel chef would be preparing the menus, Claude suggested that his small truck be used to pick up the supplies so proper selection could be made and sufficient amount kept on hand. Von Stulpnagel agreed.

"You have coal in your warehouse, too. With winter coming and coal rationed, perhaps I can use the truck to haul that, too. You will be more comfortable here, then."

With approval granted, Claude ran his biggest truck back and forth. The Germans on the Place Vendôme had food and heat, and so did all the other occupants of the Rue Cambon.

It was, in Claude's mind, an inspired idea: a coalition of hotel men to provide a network of surveillance of Nazi movements. A dozen pair of eyes able to observe the comings and goings of the enemy brass should be of inestimable value. He was willing to head up the communications center, collect the information, and convey it to the militant French. There were rumors everywhere; clandestine groups were reported forming at every point on the map. The stirring lyrics and martial tones of *La Marseillaise* had become a morning prayer for millions.

There were, also, more and more electrifying reports on the BBC from London, forbidden radio broadcasts that everyone heard, about the legendary "Charles the Tall," the indomitable General who would never surrender. Claude had already classified him as he did all French military men: "He is no Bonaparte."

The illicit broadcasts over BBC urged Frenchmen to be cautious, hold their fire, and wait for the command to rise. But Claude was impatient and decided he would begin at once to recruit the men he considered necessary to his plans.

German storm troopers were painfully in sight, silent automatons with freezing eyes, in the lobby of the Hôtel George V, as Claude crossed it to meet with his counterpart there, François Dupré.

Greetings began with customary Gallic warmth—an embrace, kisses on both cheeks—then settled into a wary exchange of views. Claude allowed Dupré to spark the early conversation, and because of the direction it took, he barely hinted why he was there.

Dupré was convinced that the Germans would remain in France and predicted that neither he nor Claude would ever see their departure in their lifetimes. For that reason, nothing could be gained by Frenchmen who wished to continue the fight. For himself, he was going to refrain from covert actions. He informed Claude that he had information the racetracks would soon reopen, and when they did he planned to make certain rich Germans his partners in a racing stable. He advised Claude to follow the same path, join them. It could only be a matter of time before England gave up and Europe settled down. The wealthy would swarm into Paris and bring big business to the hotels. "When your opponent has you by the balls," he said, "move closer to him."

Claude wasn't confiding any of his intentions to Blanche,

but she noted how he mentioned one evening that he would never speak to Dupré again or set foot in the Hôtel George V. He evaded her questions and changed the subject to the reopening of horse racing at Auteuil. The Boche was going to need to provide more than afternoons at the racetrack to take the minds of Parisians off the occupation, he said.

To Claude's surprise and anger, the first oppressive measures against Jews originated with the government at Vichy, headed by eighty-four-year-old Marshal Henri Philippe Pétain. The old man had been his commanding officer in World War I, and Claude had thought highly of him. Now he exclaimed, "A man his age should possess wisdom, but he has only acquired a weakness for insanity!"

Jews were ordered to register with the police. New directives proliferated swiftly, also expanding the definition of what made a man or woman a Jew. Had the Germans known Claude was living with a Jewess, he would automatically have been subject to the same restrictions, which included being barred from restaurants. It was certainly from the heart when he complimented her on her foresight in acquiring her false passport. She made no move to declare herself to the police.

Gabrielle Chanel had closed her fashion house and intended to keep it closed "for the duration," stating that it was due to lack of materials she required. She was living in the hotel, and soon after the Vichy Laws were posted, she ran into Claude and Blanche.

Electricity was being conserved, so the hotel's elevators were locked tight; they were trudging up the stairs.

Stopping to catch her breath, Chanel said idly, "One of my salesgirls told me you are a Jewess, Blanche."

Claude, suspecting the designer of anti-Semitism, became tense.

"You can't prove you're Jewish can you?" she asked, smiling.

"No," said Blanche, smiling in return.

"That's what I thought. I told the girl that," purred Chanel, and then they went on.

German hatred for Jews was so rabid it actually aided Jews

142

to escape them. The anti-Semites were blinded because their caricaturists went overboard with exaggeration. They portrayed the Jew as a hook-nosed, paunchy fellow in a great coat, hands clasped behind his back, his jet black hair either pushed under a hat that resembled an inverted bowl or hanging in tangled curls to his neck. To them, the Jewess was a scrawny, hollow-eyed creature with a pinched face and weepy eyes.

Provincial German soldiers received an indelible impression that all Jews were like that, and after some cartoonists placed horns sprouting on the back of a Jew's head, there were instances where youths ran their hands through the hair of arrested Jews, seeking the sensation of feeling such bumps.

In occupied France, where language difference was an additional barrier, many Jews escaped capture simply because they didn't look like the Nazi image of the Jew. So Claude could be thankful again that Blanche didn't "look Jewish." But that didn't stop him from constant apprehensions.

Significantly, he wasn't confiding in her what he hoped to do, but she didn't confide in him, either.

She didn't mean to get into it. She wasn't looking. She simply wanted to find Lily, whom she hadn't seen for months. She was just looking for her.

It never occurred to Claude that Blanche would get mixed up in the resistance movement. It had to be the farthest thing from his mind, because if he was unable to contact anyone in it, it was inconceivable that she could do it.

ABOVE: "Blanche is a perfect wife," said Claude. (*Courtesy Carolyn Robbins.*) BELOW: An associate said, "Claude has two loves, his wife and his hotel." (*Courtesy Charley Ritz.*)

RIGHT: Sir Harrison Hughes (shown here with Lady Anne Hughes, atop Notre-Dame Cathedral) was friendly to Claude and charmed by Blanche. (*Courtesy Anne Hughes.*) BELOW: Millionairess Barbara Hutton and Prince Alexis Mdvani leaving the hotel after their wedding party. (*The Bettmann Archive.*)

ABOVE LEFT: Newspaper
tycoon Lord Northcliffe
successfully substituted
as a room clerk. RIGHT:
J. Pierpont Morgan had
to have a suite that
overlooked the garden.
LEFT: Claude wouldn't
let Elsie de Wolfe
decorate the apartment.
*(Photos courtesy Culver
Pictures.)*

LEFT: Cole Porter wrote that "Even Pekinese in the Ritz do it." (*Academy of Motion Picture Arts & Sciences.*) ABOVE: Actress Fanny Ward was panicked by middle age. (*Culver Pictures.*) BELOW: Anita Loos, creator of Lorelei Lee, was a devotee of the hotel. (*Courtesy Anita Loos.*)

ABOVE: The large man, dead center, is General Karl Heinrich von Stulpnagel, who ruled occupied Paris from the Ritz. LEFT: Parisian celebrants await the victorious Allies. (*Photos courtesy G. D. Hackett.*)

RIGHT: Charley Ritz
went after fish that rose
to the surface. . . .
(*Courtesy Charley Ritz.*)
BELOW: His friend
Ernest Hemingway
went after thóse in the
deep. (*Courtesy Allen H.
Miner.*)

ABOVE: Blanche and the author confer in Paris. LEFT: Blanche and Claude—their last picture. (*Photos courtesy Jean Giaume.*)

Blanche's portrait, through which she stabbed an icepick.

12

"For me, this war is biggest thing. All after it my future will be how-you-say anti-climax."
—Lily Kharmayeff

In war, Claude considered himself a graduate *cum laude*. He had acquired the basics on the winning side in one, and a degree of expertise with the loser in his second or post-graduate war. He had taken the full curriculum.

It was with reason, therefore, that he was fearful. Thoughtful and philosophic all his life, he likened the riptides of war to those of the oceans, engulfing all who were caught in them. In such a surf, he claimed, men and women behave like children—the rising breakers enliven some by the sheer thrill of danger, while others see only the power that can destroy them. Too, there was menace in a calm; distant whitecaps could build and crest and finally crash down with all the known calamities. Settling back into the hotel, he intended to protect the two objects closest to his heart, for he had never faltered in his devotion to them both. But on a night when Blanche could not be found, he discovered it was no longer an equal division. She was everything.

It had been months since she had had news of her family. Friends she had known and loved in Paris were gone, and she was restless with a need for someone.

In the spring of 1941, the desire to know what became of Lily grew stronger in her as the confinements of the occupation hung heavier over her. She hadn't heard from "the character," as she fondly thought of her, since the Spanish civil war.

"Call it instinct or what you like, but I was sure she was in Paris. It was a feeling, an absolute certainty."

She crossed the Boulevard des Capucines, curiously devoid of traffic or noise, and went back to where Lily lived. She hit a

145

button outside the entrance, and it buzzed and a door opened. She was going toward the stairs when an elderly woman emerged from a rear apartment to ask what she wanted.

The woman was maddeningly slow after Blanche gave her Lily's name and described her appearance. She went into a virtual trance, holding all ten fingers to her closed eyes as if that would provide a parade of tenants past and present to her view. While Blanche waited, another woman came out of the same rear apartment. She was younger but equally obtuse. Blanche had a problem making her understand the most simple terms, and it took a long time before they decided they couldn't help her.

Anyone better versed in the use of stupidity as a delaying tactic would have been suspicious much earlier. Blanche spent more than a quarter of an hour with them before she gave up. She was no sooner out in the sunlight than she walked straight into the arms of two Gestapo agents.

They made a quick search of her person, one of them lingering so long around the area of her breasts that she asked, *"Na' viel vergnuegen?"* Then slapped him. The other grabbed him before he could retaliate. Blanche wasn't sure if the officer she slapped was going for his gun or his fists. The Germans shoved her across the curb to a waiting truck, then they raced away from a silent gathering of spectators.

She was put in a cell full of females held on charges ranging from prostitution to thievery, all on the accusations of members of the invading army.

Two disconsolate girls were curled up on the floor of the cell where her captors deposited her. Neither stirred nor answered when Blanche tried to make conversation. She left them alone and began shouting demands to the guard. He was fat, his name was Herman, and his annoyance with her slowly turned into enchantment. When she complained about the cold floor, he brought in a mattress and later contributed a blanket. She attributed this benevolence to his surprise and happiness on hearing her speak German and because she claimed he reminded her of her brother Herman in America, which, of course, he didn't. The girls, eyeing all this with enormous suspicion, apparently decided his largesse proved she was there to spy. They rejected all her attempts to be friendly. They wouldn't even accept her cigarettes, although Herman did. He brought her matches when hers ran out, but shrugged off her plea to make a phone call to Claude.

She spent the night with a curious feeling of equanimity, considering the circumstances. She couldn't believe anything bad would happen to her. She was taken the next morning to an interrogation. When the officer who questioned her leveled on the subject of Lily, she realized the women in the apartment building were informers; there was no other way her jailers could have known.

The interrogator, speaking English because her nationality had come to light through possession of her passport, conducted the questioning in a friendly manner. He even lit her cigarette for her, reminding her as he did that he and his countrymen were true gentlemen, and when the United States recognized the righteousness of the German cause they would surely join with them. Any day now, he told her, we could be allies.

"You should live so long," she snapped.

Thereupon he demanded she tell how she knew Lily and for how long and how well and why she was looking for her. She answered truthfully, but denied knowing any of her "comrades." After each question she asked, "Why do you want to know?" which went unanswered. Finally she said, "If I knew where she was, I wouldn't have gone looking for her, would I?"

The interrogation over, she demanded they drive her back to the Ritz. "And not in a truck!" They took her to the hotel in a swastika-marked Mercedes-Benz. Claude was on the Vendôme side at the time, frantically trying to see if anyone knew her whereabouts. He had already canvassed hospitals and the police and the few Americans he knew to be still in Paris.

It seemed, on reflection, he had suffered more than she. She had undergone no indignities and was quite intact. Claude figured that serious charges must have been made against Lily, whom he barely knew. Relieved that Blanche had innocently walked into trouble, he cautioned her that she was risking her freedom and possibly her life if she attempted to find the girl again.

"I hope this terrible experience has been a lesson to you."

"There was nothing terrible about it," she said. "In fact, I wouldn't have missed it for the world!"

Dupré was only the first of several managers with no desire to go along with Claude's surveillance of the Germans under his roof. The manager of the Continental, whose premises were virtually staff headquarters, had army men bedded in five hundred rooms and was more inclined to resignation than resistance. He was a terribly harassed man, almost weeping under strain. By the armistice terms, all hotel rooms, regardless of their size, that were occupied by Germans were being paid for by the French government at a set rate of 25 francs a day. (Then equivalent to about sixty cents, American money.) Officially, however, Adolf Hitler was their host. By edict, every German in Paris was "A guest of der Führer."

From the Continental it was a short walk to the Crillon, where the manager also begged off participation. He pleaded with Claude to be sympathetic to the plight of his contemporaries. With Germans peering over their shoulders, their own movements would be all too visible. He would go part way, however, and keep his eyes open and drop into the Ritz from time to time if he had something to report. "But," he remarked, "it is useless to keep one's eyes open after his head has been chopped off."

The manager of the Plaza Athénée was equally disinclined, preferring to maintain the *status quo* until the situation cleared.

Claude cut down his visits to other hotels. He had seen only men known to him. Disaster would certainly befall him should anyone tip off the enemy as to his intentions.

Then, unexpectedly, he was contacted by a member of a group formulating plans for active resistance. One of the managers Claude had tried to recruit sent Martin to him. The clouds of secrecy that enveloped every conspiratorial move against the enemy hardly lifted, however, for Martin refused to identify who sent him or even supply statistical information about himself.

After a few wary meetings, Claude decided that "although I thought at first he was a scoundrel," Martin was entirely trustworthy. By then he knew enough about him to realize that the good-looking, self-assured fellow's acquaintanceship with women provided clues to his calling. Prewar, he had been a popular, desirable gigolo.

In war he had a new direction, agent for a group passing on messages to freedom fighters specializing in the harassment of German troops. There were sharpshooters and dynamiters among them. Martin looked forward to the day Claude's information would provide them with the chance to assassinate some Nazi bigwig in transit.

They began by devising code names couched in words related to the needs of the hotel, mainly food and kitchen staples most likely to be required. As they worked on that, Hermann Goering checked in from Berlin, taking a suite previously occupied by kings, merchant princes and heiresses. It contained two huge salons, six bedrooms and four bathrooms. Stulpnagel officially decreed it had to be called the Hermann Goering Suite henceforth and forever. While the corpulent Reichsmarshal was expressing delight with the luxury that was his, the two conspirators were deciding his code name would be "Potato."

Meetings between Claude and Martin were conducted openly during this phase of their association, Martin posing as a salesman for various suppliers. With the Germans continuing their efforts to rule Paris under mild restrictions, there seemed little reason for apprehension. Claude's greatest worry was that Blanche would discover what he was doing. He carefully hid his actions from her, while she was carefully hiding hers from him.

Conversations in the salons of the Ritz dealt largely with stories of Nazi looting, especially of apartments left unoccupied by owners gone abroad. Claude had no worry about their possessions on the Avenue Montaigne. It was enough that Elise, the housekeeper, remained. He warned Blanche to stay away from there. "You are too risk-prone," he said. His concern after her overnight incarceration was plain, an indication of his love. It touched her and immobilized her—for a week.

Then she felt a need to see for herself that everything in the apartment was intact, so she went. There had been no visitations; the housekeeper was living with her daughter in splendid isolation.

As Blanche started back to the Ritz, the proprietor of a sweets shop, an old man, rushed out. He made a great show of happiness at seeing her again. "You are English, yes?"

He insisted she come in and accept a gift of newly arrived Swiss chocolates, then ushered her to the rear, where he brought a young boy out of hiding. A Royal Air Force gunner, he had parachuted from his crippled plane into a meadow near Abbeville the last day of fighting. It took weeks for his wounds to heal; then the French had passed him on toward Paris, where he was to be handed over to a resistance movement that would attempt to send him home via Spain or Marseilles. Although he came down close to the Channel, escape in that direction was completely bottled up; not even a rowboat could go out to sea from the north French coast without inspection by German patrols.

The boy was thin, wasted and frightened. When she spoke, even though it was only to say she had no idea what she could do for him, he was happily overcome by the sound of one with whom he could communicate.

A cousin of the proprietor was in the shop, too. The boy had knocked on his door in the middle of the night, after waiting in vain for a resistance contact who never appeared. The strain of having him on their hands only a few hours was telling on both Frenchmen; it showed in their excited appeals to Blanche to get the fugitive out of the place quickly. When she repeated that she had no idea how, they slapped their hands on their sides expressively and glared at her. In that case, they had no alternative but to turn him over to the Germans.

She telephoned Claude, who hung up savagely when she began to make clear her reason for calling. She was talking it

150

over with the boy, trying to figure his next move, when the hotel's small pickup truck dropped off a furtive little man and scooted away. It was Greep, the Levantine forger who had supplied her doctored passport. Following her emergency call, Claude had discovered a tie to the resistance from a bartender in his own hotel.

Happily for the shopkeeper and his cousin, Greep wanted to get started at once. He declared there were German sentries to pass on his route and they might prove troublesome after dark. He was going to take the boy to a barge on the Seine, moored near the Pont d'Austerlitz.

"You've done it before?" Blanche asked.

He had not. This was his first, but a close friend had shown him how one handled it.

"Where is he?"

The Levantine laughed. "Ask the Boche!" He thought it a good joke. His friend had failed to return from a recent assignment.

She delayed their departure, pondering the options. Greep's English was dismal, his French fractured, his German blank. "If a sentry speaks to you, what do you do?"

"We run," he said, and laughed again.

She informed Greep she would escort the boy. That was okay with him; he identified the barge. "Eet is a nest for creepled peegeons," he said. A pair of pigeons caged on deck provided the symbol of recognition.

Alone with the boy, she appraised his blond hair and fair Anglo-Saxon skin that would help him pass as German. His ill-fitting pants, shirt and jacket would do, although she would have preferred something better. His weakened look would help win sympathy if they were stopped. That fitted the role she wanted him to play, a recovering invalid taking a prescribed afternoon constitutional with a domineering German nurse who would brook no interference from a common soldier.

"When I speak to you, just nod your head and say, '*Ja wohl*.'" She made him say it until she approved his pronunciation. Then she advised him he must look directly at soldiers

151

and even smile a greeting at them. She was author, director and star of the show, and as they made their way to the river in the streets and the reopened Métro, the journey became positively exhilarating.

She left him with the barge in sight and returned to the Ritz. It was a marvelous adventure, one she would later refer to as "The Pigeon Safari."

Claude was pacing up and down, frustrated and furious. He intended to administer the "supreme chastisement" to his errant wife the moment she appeared, but when she breezed through the door and embraced him, tears formed in his eyes. Nearby, Marie Louise Ritz, as stern as Blanche had ever seen her, stalked away without a word.

The "supreme chastisement" materialized when they were in their rooms. She had disobeyed, scared the wits out of him, put her life on the line, and might still bring down the wrath of the enemy if the boy, the shopkeeper or his cousin divulged what had transpired.

"The boy doesn't know anything about me," she said. "And that shopkeeper and his cousin won't talk; they'll drop dead from fright before they do."

"See here, Blanchette, I know how bright you are, but there are times I wonder if you have all your brains together."

"Popsy, you'd have done the same thing if you'd been there. You'd never let that nice kid go with that idiot."

"No. I am an idiot to believe your promises. Now, look here, if it happens again, I will send you to New York. You are neutral, an American, you know. I can do it."

Repercussions came from Marie Louise, who summoned him to her salon on the top floor. The yapping of the dogs subsided when he came in and kissed her hand. She was seated in a dim light near the window, her spectacles low on her nose, a half-completed petit-point pillow-cover on her knees. Its colors matched other examples of her skill visible on chairs and the window seat.

"Monsieur Auzello," she said, then stopped as if she had run out of breath. She looked out the window. They had used

152

"Monsieur Auzello" and "Madame Ritz" with each other from the first day they met, and it would always be that way.

"Monsieur Auzello, I must speak to you about your wife. The actions of Madame Auzello jeopardize the hotel, and you, and me as well."

"Blanche meant well," he told her. "What happened was accidental. It won't happen again."

"But you? What about you? I know your feelings; I don't approve."

"And I understand your position, Madame Ritz. You are Swiss. But I can't be neutral about the captivity of my country. You would rather I resign?"

"NO! I need you more than ever." She sighed deeply. "Our world is upside-down; it will never be right again. Chanel is leaving us now."

"I know. But she will be back."

"Perhaps. But I wonder. She is going to live in Switzerland, indefinitely. She asked that I go with her. It is easy to run away."

She saw a look come into his eyes and shook her head. "Don't worry, how can I? I won't leave my hotel while the Germans are here unless I die. That's why I need you—to help me preserve what's left, for whatever comes."

"But of course, Madame Ritz."

"I trust you, whatever you do, but especially to protect the hotel. If you don't, if you arouse the Germans and they destroy this, my husband's masterpiece—you know they are capable of it—then . . ." She managed to smile before she finished the sentence.

Blanche had concerns of her own with Claude's attitude toward the Germans. He told her he would die before he touched the hand of a Nazi, and when he came face to face with von Stulpnagel in the lobby he very nearly proved it. The military commander of Paris recognized him and held out his hand. Claude bowed slightly and turned away.

Blanche called it stupid.

"Dangerous perhaps, but not stupid," he said.

The General had withdrawn his hand and gone on. "He understood," said Claude.

"Ha! How many times have you told me they are 'cold-hearted animals'? Your own words! 'Be careful, Blanche. Their uniform gives them a license to kill.' That's what you said. And yet, every time you see one you practically dare him to blow your head off!"

So she was worried about him, and so was Marie Louise Ritz. A few days later he suggested that Hans Elmiger take over the managerial relationship with their Nazi residents. Marie Louise congratulated him for delegating the authority to his quiet, relaxed assistant, and Elmiger quickly proved his resourcefulness at the job.

The Germans were in the process of checking the Ritz cellars where, traditionally, regular guests stored trunks. They were curious about their contents and not averse to seizing anything of value. To get to them, they had to pass racks containing bottles of rare wines in plain view. Elmiger accompanied the search party, and the inevitable happened. The group stopped dead at the sight of the liquid treasures, their intentions plain.

Indicating the bottles, Elmiger said, "We must be careful not to disturb these. They are the property of Reichsmarshal Goering!" The wines remained undisturbed.

When Goering took off for Germany, Claude ruefully forwarded the bill for housing him to the government accounting office. Payment for the Reichsmarshal's suite, accruing to the hotel, came to just over ten dollars a day. Normally it was in the thousand-dollar-a-week range.

Soon after that, Martin appeared to find out why Claude had failed to notify him of enemy comings and goings. It forced Claude into agonizing soul-searching.

"I must be loyal to the hotel," he told the underground agent. "Look here, if we create an incident, it could spread far beyond Place Vendôme. It would finish me, but that is of no importance. The murder of one of these Nazis—perhaps Goering—even though it would be a shot fired in our own cause, could ricochet against us all; yes, I truly believe it could make Hitler order the destruction not only of the Ritz but of all of France!"

During that first year of the occupation, Blanche and Claude settled into a kind of survival routine. Everything associated with their previous lifestyles had changed.

To pass the time, now that they were completely cut off from the elegant hours they had known, Blanche and Maggy Fahmi-Bey organized bridge games at Maggy's apartment and, when enough players were available, poker. "We played almost every day," said Blanche, "and I would have been bored stiff except that I kept on winning."

Claude saw to it that the Ritz functioned as well as possible in its segregated way. The first winter of the occupation was the coldest he could remember, but by keeping the hotel heated with German coal and continuing to offer low rates to honeymooners, the Cambon half remained busy. There was more activity on that side than on the Place Vendôme side.

There, however, almost everyone was in uniform. Claude's former office was being used as a checkroom for sidearms, machine guns and ammunition. On duty in it, guards waited for emergency signals that never sounded. The atmosphere throughout the hotel was so relaxed that when a bartender called the inactive months before the blitzkrieg a sitzkrieg, Blanche suggested the current period be called the Ritzkrieg. Nobody laughed.

That calm and quiet came to an end late in June 1941. Suddenly the military personnel on the Vendôme side stirred into a frenzy of activity. Machine guns were dragged out and set up with gunners beside them, trigger fingers at the ready. Storm troopers in black uniforms, wearing death's head insignia, took positions outside Stulpnagel's office. The halls reverberated with shouted commands, marching boots, heel clicks and cocked guns, sounds like music to soldiers when the killings begin.

The fear for their lives surfaced when Hitler abruptly turned on Russia. Until then, Communists, outlawed in

France, had taken no active role in the war. But their reputation for terroristic activity conjured up the specter of murderers on the loose; paranoia sent a shudder of shock waves against the walls of the Ritz.

A new warning was added to the German edicts in circulation. Anyone currently in jail could become a hostage subject to the death sentence if criminal acts were perpetrated against members of the occupying forces. While posters proclaiming this were being plastered around Paris, a German naval officer running to catch a subway train in the Pigalle area was shot dead. Across town, in another Métro station, an officer of the army was killed. Coming closer to the Ritz, a grenade was tossed into the lobby of a hotel near Boulevard Haussmann that served as residence for a number of Germans. All responsible for these actions escaped, but twenty men in prison for less violent activities did not; General von Stulpnagel ordered them executed.

Before the war, Blanche had constantly received bouquets from acquaintances, admirers and friends. They betokened various forms of devotion, some of them sincere. Since September 1939, there had been none of any kind.

In November 1941, a small boy brought a tender bouquet of violets to the desk on the Rue Cambon side and asked to be allowed to hand them to her. It was a very small gift, nothing like the roses, gardenias or orchids of memory. There was no card—the donor was anonymous—but the boy let slip that he often saw the lady who sent the violets around the stall where he worked in the Marché aux Fleurs.

Blanche knew immediately that Lily wanted to see her.

13

"Love does more harm than good, and God would do men a favor if he rid us of it forever."
—Napoleon Bonaparte

She moved through the lanes, lush with autumn flowers, peering into stalls on both sides, stopping where boxes of violets were displayed.

Lily saw her first, which was fortunate because Blanche might not have recognized her. Her hair was cropped close to her face and hugged the top of her head; it made her look more like a cute boy. "I would have known her, I think," said Blanche, "because of her smile and her eyes."

But Lily had already flown at her, smothering her in an embrace and repeating over and over, "I know you come."

"If you felt this way, why did you wait so long?" Blanche asked severely.

"Is long story and not so good one. But now is okay." She hugged Blanche again and whispered, "Is necessary nobody hear me what I say." She signaled she was leaving to a tall youth watching from a distance, and they went to the quai, where she pounced upon an unoccupied bench.

"From now," she said, "you come meet me here, yes?" She set the topography of the bench, pointing to a bookstore across the way and a splash of paint dabbed on the grey wall behind.

Then she launched into an excited account of new friends in her life. She talked fast and got her syntax and grammar garbled. Blanche couldn't be sure of everything she said, except that she figured in Lily's plans.

"My friends is very nice peoples. You will like him very much. From Hotel Ritz for sure you bring me ration cards and cigarettes and sometimes foods, certainly. You say me yes?"

"If I can. But why?"

157

Lily looked at her in disbelief. "I just tell you. We make life bad for Germans, maybe kill."

It was Blanche's turn to show disbelief.

"You say me yes, Blanche?"

"No, I don't think I can. In fact, you'd better not count on it."

She could have saved her breath.

"I know. Always you need time to arrange. When you see me tomorrow, I bring Vincenzo and he makes better explain. I see you twelve o'clock, yes."

Then she darted away, leaving Blanche to think it over and decide she would not come back the next day or even consider helping Lily's friends wage a private war.

She had lunch in her room the next day, expecting Lily to phone, ready to explain she could not participate. Later, when there was no call, she went over to Maggy's apartment to play cards. There was no message when she returned to the hotel.

On the third day, another bunch of violets was left at the desk for her. She went directly to the bench, and in a few moments Lily appeared with Vincenzo. He was the fellow she had seen at the flower market. He shook hands, then sat down on the other side of Lily and placed a caressing arm around her. He was younger, well educated, French with an Italian name and a good command of English.

Blanche told how she tried to find Lily and was arrested. They listened attentively, nodding their heads and smiling broadly.

"Thees womens they walk two sides of street," said Lily. "We knows."

"I don't think they know what a dangerous game they're in," said Vincenzo. "Sooner or later, it will be us or the Germans who see they get theirs."

"Maybe I do," said Lily. "With my own two hands. Like thees."

She put her hands around Vincenzo's neck, and he rolled his eyes and put out his tongue and pretended he was strangled. Then both laughed heartily.

"Good clean fun," thought Blanche. It didn't seem possible

they had serious intentions, so she didn't feel called upon to say that Claude would never let her get involved with them. It seemed to her that Vincenzo realized at once that she wouldn't go along; he was silent, at times he shook Lily's shoulder as if to make her understand how Blanche felt. But Lily went on without noticing him.

"You have the American passport, yes? You have the language, yes, I know, German, too. We give you paper for French and German, and each one is for different person."

Finally Vincenzo interrupted. "We don't expect you to come in with us unless you want to. And if you do, we will be careful that you know what we're doing and how you are part of it."

"Yes," burst in Lily. "Just like I have explain already to you!"

"There was no rationale for my getting mixed up in it," said Blanche later. "There were plenty of good reasons why I shouldn't." The most prominent was her need to deceive Claude, for she was determined he mustn't know. But with curfew in stringent force, her meetings with Lily's group were during daylight hours, when, Claude believed blissfully, she was playing bridge or poker or at tea parties and *kaffeeklatsches* with other women, sitting out the lengthening and tiresome occupation.

Sitting in with Lily and her friends did much to enliven her days. "They were the most disorganized people," she said. "Some that they talked about I never got to meet, but those I did were having a marvelous time. It took me a while to realize they were serious partisans and not just a bunch of kids playing hide and seek."

The least amusing, Heifer, was the dedicated one. The fat girl from Lily's earlier crowd was a fiery revolutionary, thrown into a shock of confusion when Hitler and Stalin became allies. However, when the Nazis turned on Russia, they helped sort out her loyalties. She was the most zealous of all in her determination to wipe the German army out of France.

Lily and Heifer engaged in furious spats over the *modus operandi,* quarrels that Vincenzo watched with amused tolerance. "Lily came closest to being their leader," said Blanche,

159

"although everybody was a general. Except me. Yet if I had decided to give orders, they would have obeyed me, too."

Vincenzo took pains to protect the identity of the members in their group who were reluctant to make themselves known. "But we are all in danger, and I feel you should know."

Their purpose, he told her, was to secure information and get it to field units. "We want you to pick up certain messages here and there; some you bring to us, others must be taken places we will give you. Are you willing?"

She said, "Sure. I'll try."

Heifer and Vincenzo would be performing the same duties, but Lily was in restraint—her name was on an active list of those wanted by the Nazis. "It is not easy to hold her down," lamented Vincenzo.

Lily smiled. "Except in the bed."

Like a skittish pony whose wildness could result in self-destruction, Lily wanted to shake off the reins imposed for her own protection.

She had a strong reason for hating Germans. Her former lover, Robert, had been picked up in a sweep of the student quarter during the first week of the occupation. He was still being held when orders came through to execute random prisoners as a reprisal measure.

"That was the end of Robert," Lily told Blanche with controlled emotion. She had learned about it when she saw his name among the dead on placards posted around the city. She broke down and was nursed back to health by Vincenzo, who stepped in to fill the gap in her life. He kept her hidden from the Nazis who were looking for her and, inadvertently, from Blanche who was doing the same. He, too, was a devoted lover, but to Lily, Robert was special. In spirit, Robert was always with her.

The first mission that Vincenzo entrusted to Blanche was to take a lunch pail to a railway worker at the Gare du Nord. He instructed her that she must arrive precisely at 1400 hours.

He handed over a French identity card with the name Berthé Valéry and showed her a snapshot of a dour-looking Frenchman she should call Moule. "He is your husband." He

160

would be waiting at Track 5 and would berate her for being late with his lunch.

She went into the back of the stall, changed into a cheap cotton dress, rumpled her hairdo, and removed her makeup. When she was ready to go, he said, "I will not hide from you that what you will be doing is very dangerous. You are carrying microfilm with photographs of documents stolen from German headquarters. They give the position of gun emplacements along the coast, and the Germans are moving heaven and earth to find them. So if you are caught, it will go hard with you."

He advised her to get out of the terminal as soon as she handed the pail to Moule, who would hide the microfilm in a hotbox of a car bound for Calais, where it would be delivered to a British intelligence agent. "I said I would tell you all you are asked to do, so now you know. Maybe you don't want to do it?"

She said, "I can do with some excitement."

But on the way to the terminal she started shaking, her stomach was turning over, and she felt she could kick herself. "I told myself I wasn't brave, just stupid. Why am I doing this?"

Thinking it over as she made her way across Paris, it struck her that it was impossible for Vincenzo to entrust her with such a vital mission the first time out. It didn't make sense for him to tell her everything. What if she were caught or tortured? Her disclosures could destroy them all. He seemed to have gone out of his way to frighten her. Suddenly she saw it all. She was being tested; there was no microfilm.

With a lightened heart, she went through the huge terminal, presenting Berthé Valéry's identity card to uniformed French gendarmes and German soldiers. They waved her through the barrier to Track 5, where Moule was looking for her. He came forward scowling, feigning anger that she had made him wait for his lunch. Nearby, two Germans on patrol in the huge and smoky structure watched them with broad grins.

"Moule made it look absolutely real," she said. "So, as I was supposed to be his wife, I grabbed him and gave him a passionate kiss on the lips. He was so surprised he dropped the lunch pail, which reminded me of the time I built up my part at Fort Lee. Everything fell on the floor then, too. But this time it went just fine. One of the Germans thought it was great—when I stepped back he applauded. The other one called out, 'Vive la France.' I guess the nature of the country was getting to them."

Amused by this charade she had participated in, she went back to the market. Vincenzo was waiting for her. He praised her for performing so well under pressure. She expected him to reveal the truth then. She hoped he would, for, after all, she had passed the test with flying colors. But he didn't say a word about it, so she went behind the stall, changed her clothes, reinstated her cosmetics, and fixed her hair. While doing that, she heard Lily's voice, unusually shrill, raging at Vincenzo.

When she stepped out, Lily's fury had grown into a full-scale physical attack; she was flailing away at the young giant. A long scratch near his eyes had drawn blood, and while he was holding her then at arm's length, she was kicking furiously at his ankles. Flower vendors and a few late-afternoon customers were watching, amused at what they assumed to be a lovers' quarrel.

At the sight of Blanche, a sulking Vincenzo stalked off to tend his wounds and a subdued Lily burst into tears in the cane chair he unceremoniously shoved her into.

After the last onlooker drifted away, she said to Blanche, "For why you do what he say?"

"Didn't you want me to?"

"Hah! You think I want you be dead? Why you think Heifer run away today?"

"You mean, it really was all he said?"

"How I know what he says? He send me away on false goose chase while you take life in hands. Why he no do it himself? Why he no ask me? You know why? If caught, you be dead! I tell you thees absolutely!"

She returned to the Ritz, went straight to her room, and stayed there. When Claude appeared and she refused to go downstairs with him to dinner, he asked if she had lost a lot of money at cards.

"No," she said, and added enigmatically, "In a way, I came out a winner."

There were no more violets. Lily told her it had never been her intention to include her in dangerous activities. "Black market, maybe. Is fun. All do it, even Germans. For me, is different.

"For me, this war is biggest thing. All after it my future will be how-you-say anti-climax."

A few weeks later, on a cold December night, Claude was awakened by a low rap on the door of their room.

He donned his robe and had a few words with an unseen man who held his mouth close to the crack opened for him. Afterward, he sat on the edge of the bed in deep thought.

"Get in bed," Blanche commanded. "You'll catch cold." He crawled in beside her but tossed restlessly. Finally she turned on the light and looked at him.

He said, "You mustn't speak of this when you go downstairs in the morning. Be surprised when someone tells you. The Japanese have bombed an American naval base in Hawaii. There are heavy casualties. Your country will be in the war before morning. You have become an enemy alien now."

"What do you think I've been up to now?"

The calendar had moved only into February 1942 when the Gestapo appeared and took Claude away. Hotel personnel stood around and gaped; there was nothing they could do about it. He was hustled out with no time to gather any belongings, and nobody knew why he was seized.

A phone call to the room summoned Blanche downstairs, and when she was told what had happened she ran around to the Vendôme side. There she learned that Erich Ebert had been transferred. His replacement stolidly turned away her questions about the arrest. Another aide to von Stulpnagel told her the General had no jurisdiction over actions of the secret police. They ordered her to leave.

She threw some clothes into a suitcase and took it to the

163

Cherche-Midi Prison, because that was where she had been held. Guards took it away from her and carried it inside, but ignored questions as to whether Claude was there.

Desolate and alone, she went to a nearby corner café and sat at a sidewalk table drinking a double cognac. She could barely look at the bleak building, it depressed her so. Although the drink stimulated her, she had no idea what to do next; it seemed to her that her brain had stopped functioning.

The low rap on the door that had awakened Claude the night when the United States came into the war sounded again. The man who spoke had turned off the hall illumination. Faceless, he told her, in a muffled voice, that Claude was in Cherche-Midi, which was a good sign.

"When they are taken to Fresnes—"

He didn't finish that sentence.

"What has he done?" she asked.

"He has been accused of helping Communists."

"What?"

"Last week Radio Moscow thanked him."

"He's no Communist!"

No response. Then: "Maybe they will let him out soon." He moved off in the dark, and she sat the rest of the night in the big chair that Claude had used when he read his books and newspapers. She sat for three hours, mentally sifting all the angles open to her. She examined every person she knew in Paris who might help her. Lily, Greep, Madame Ritz, the barmen and the concierges, but when morning came she decided she, alone, must take the actions that the situation required. As to what they were, she didn't have the slightest idea.

Late the next afternoon, distraught and still lacking inspiration, she went to the lobby. To her surprise a stranger rose from a divan, came up to her, and said, "Mrs. Auzello, I am a friend of your husband. You may have heard him mention me. I am Martin."

He was looking hard at her, and she responded with a loud "Of course. How nice to see you."

"Perhaps we can promenade," he said.

She went back upstairs and bundled herself up in a sweater and heavy overcoat.

They went out, crossed the Rue de Rivoli, making banal observations about the weather, which was windy and cheerless. It was even colder in the open Tuileries, but she let him guide her there. Even then, he said nothing significant.

The strain was telling on the suave young man who had been so self-assured when he first made himself known to Claude. He kept a wary eye on the few people in sight and pulled nervously on the right side of his mustache, mannerisms that upset her.

Satisfied at last that they were not being watched, he handed her an ink-soiled clandestine paper, mimeographed by a Paris resistance group. It was literate and professional in tone.

Claude's name appeared among Frenchmen newly jailed at Cherche-Midi. Alongside his name was a paragraph deriding his captors. "It is a case of bungling on both sides of the Eastern front. Radio Moscow is gloating over its assumption that a Communist (Auzello) was operating a famous capitalistic hotel while here in Paris. The simple Teutonic souls, who quiver with fright as they seek to rule France, believe everything the Russians say."

Blanche handed back the pages, saying she no longer cared why he was in—all she wanted was to get him out. "Can you help me?"

He shook his head. "They are interrogating him; that's all we know."

"That's what they did to me. Then they let me go."

"Perhaps they'll do the same with your husband." But his voice lacked conviction. "The Communists are giving them the most trouble now. Heinrich Himmler is reportedly here to supervise operations against them."

"What you're saying is that there is nothing I can do?"

"You can pray."

He started away, then turned back to ask if she wanted the clandestine paper before he burned it. She took it.

Even if she had been able to concentrate better, she wouldn't have been interested in the technical information about German weaponry and regiments that filled the columns. She was about to set the pages on fire when a summation of German military personalities caught her eye. Apparently a regular feature, it disclosed the background, family ties, personality traits, habits, likes and dislikes of members of the German high command. There were three, and one was Otto von Stulpnagel. She skimmed through it. One observation that registered in her consciousness was the admission that "alone among career officers in Paris, he maintains a reasonable attitude toward the populace and continues to oppose the ruthless execution of dissidents ordered by Berlin."

She tore up the pages and burned them, a difficult task in the biting wind. When the last ashes had blown away, she leaned against a wall that provided a shield, reassembling her thoughts, groping for an idea that would spur her into action.

"I took stock of myself then," she recalled, "and thought, 'My God, what the hell has happened to you? You never had to worry about doing something—you did it. You haven't the guts you had when you first came to Paris. You're all mixed up. You don't know if you're American, French, Jewish, gentile or what! Put them all together and you're nothing.

"'My God, you even let some pipsqueak on Stulpnagel's staff turn you away when you should have given him a shove and gone right through.'"

That, to the best of her recollection, was as far as she got. The next thing she knew she was marching resolutely past the protesting sentry at the Vendôme entrance of the Ritz.

This is her account of what happened then:

"I went up to the first soldier I saw and said, 'Take me to General von Stulpnagel. We have an appointment.'

"He looked startled and said, 'Who made that appointment?' I gave him a withering look and said, 'I did,' very loud and strong. He motioned me to follow him, and I did. There was another fellow upstairs, and I said, 'Tell General von Stulpnagel the wife of the Managing Directeur of this hotel is here for her appointment.'

"At that moment another soldier—it was his valet, I found out later—came along with some tea on a tray, and as he

166

started inside with the soldier who was going to announce me, I decided I might as well play my part with everything I had. So I said, 'Tell him I take cream and three lumps.'

"A few minutes later, von Stulpnagel came out and wanted to know if I had really come for tea. I told him that what I wanted was for him to give me my husband back. He said he knew Claude had been arrested, but it was a Nazi party matter and did not concern the military.

"'We are not the same,' he said.

"I sat there while he drank his tea, and finally he asked, 'What did he do?'

"'Nothing.'

"'Ahhh,' he said, smiling. 'The most common crime of all.'

"He said Claude was a good man and it was no disgrace to keep fighting your country's enemies in a war.

"I was speaking German, and he asked me if I had ever been to Berlin. I said I loved Paris too much to go there. He said Paris was the most beautiful city he had ever seen and its women were the same. He was a gentleman; I liked him. I remembered that line Claude had once used, so I said, 'I must get him back because in Paris a woman without her man in bed with her is only half a woman.'

"We didn't say much after that. He finished his tea, and I expected he would tell me to go. Instead, he said, 'I'm going to try to get your husband out!'

"He asked me to wait outside while he made a phone call. I guess it was about ten minutes, but it seemed forever. Then he came out and said, 'Good news. The charges against Monsieur Auzello are being dropped. Tonight you can be a whole woman again!'"

With that, the bravado went out of her. She was so overcome she couldn't speak. But as she stood there, fighting to keep a grip on herself, he said, "Your accent puzzles me. Where did you get it?"

"I was okay again. I looked him straight in the eye and said, 'Brooklyn, New York!'

"Then I went around to the other side of the hotel, and about ten o'clock that night they brought Claude in.

167

"He was dragging heavily, completely drained. He had been interrogated for nearly forty-eight hours straight, he said, denying Communist connections, mystified by the allegations. He kept saying, 'I am against Communism, and you cannot prove otherwise.'"

He didn't know that Blanche had interceded for his release until she told him.

"See here, I never knew you came from Brooklyn," he said.

"I don't," she said. "It seemed the right thing to say!"

A few days later she went through the Vendôme side again, feeling she owed von Stulpnagel a greater show of thanks.

He was no longer there; another Stulpnagel had replaced him. Heinrich's reputation for ruthlessness was in exact proportion to the reasonableness of his displaced cousin Otto.

14

"The last time I saw Paris
Her heart was warm and gay.
No matter how they change her,
I'll remember her that way."
—Oscar Hammerstein II

Grandeur at the Ritz was a casualty of war. In the summer of 1942, elegance was dead, destroyed by stiff restrictions and short rations. Nobody could live at the top, eat well, drink well or dress well. Fashion was nonexistent; style, what there was of it, was homemade.

Hope that the Americans with their legendary strength would arrive quickly, oust the Nazis, and restore the past soon evaporated. It was a beautiful dream, but it didn't come true.

"We were without news of family or friends," Blanche said. "From being a prisoner in a cell, I became a prisoner on a continent. But it made no difference, knowing what was happening added up to the same thing—zero."

In America, gossip reporter Walter Winchell provided family and friends with startling news about her.

In his syndicated newspaper column, he wrote:

"Blanche Auzello, American wife of the Managing Directeur of the Paris Ritz, has been executed by the Nazis!"

Similar items, labeled *Exclusives from Inside Occupied Europe*, appeared in his writings or were scattered like buckshot in his Sunday-night radio broadcasts. He delivered them in a vivid staccato style, so positively that no one raised doubts about their veracity:

"Pals are worried by fashion leader Gabrielle Chanel's disappearance! . . . Ruth Dubonnet, wife of liquor tycoon André Dubonnet, has hidden her American birth from Nazi nasties by flushing her passport down the toilet! . . . Gertrude Stein is working as a cook in a Montmartre hashery!"

Winchell refused all pleas for further details, piously claiming he always protected his sources. But ultimately it was re-

169

vealed that his information came from Elsa Maxwell, then a guest of friends at such well-known resorts inside Europe as Southampton, Palm Beach and Beverly Hills.

The sound from America that penetrated the Ritz was the drone of bombers high in the night skies. Each week it grew louder and took longer to pass, because more planes were flying. Claude told Blanche they were manned by the British but made in the U.S.A. He had heard it on the BBC, the most listened-to voice in Europe. Life in London was as hard as in Paris, except they didn't have Nazi soldiers at the Ritz in Piccadilly.

In France, the Germans had torn away the mask of friendship they had brought with them. Heinrich von Stulpnagel made the soldiers on the Vendôme side goose-step in a lively fashion. The crunch of their boots on César Ritz's treasured floors could be heard clear across the hotel.

The underground, still disorganized and in disconnected groups, was inflicting hurts with guerilla tactics, hit-and-run bombings, and assassinations. The stepped-up activity affected Blanche and Claude, for each knew, now, that the other had been involved in the clandestine war. Blanche worried for Claude and Claude for Blanche.

He applied for visas to cross the demarcation line to see his mother. "I'd rather stay here," Blanche told him. Her relationship with seventy-four-year-old Melinda Auzello had never improved.

With her usual self-assurance, Lily strode into the hotel and went to Blanche's rooms. She had things to relate about Heifer. When they became clear after much excited explanation, Blanche called Claude to hear them.

The fat girl had been arrested by the Nazis and identified as a member of the Maquis Rouge, partisans allied to the left-wing National Front. Questioned and tortured, she made a number of admissions.

When Claude asked how Lily knew this, she smiled mysteriously. "Many German mans like many French mans walk two sides of street. Yes, Blanche knows, not always mans, womans too! Many do it."

Heifer's confession had included the name Auzello among fellow conspirators, and her captors assumed Claude was the person she meant, not Blanche. That accounted for his arrest and tie to the Communists.

"You never know the suffer I have for Blanche when thees Germans man tells me all that Heifer do. Then I hear it is the Monsieur Auzello they take and I am happy again. I know you sure be okay, like you see now."

When the visa to the south was granted, Claude overrode her objections. "Look here, you are going with me. I will not leave you here in Paris, especially not with that Lily. And I tell you now, you are not to see her again. It is finished!"

"Don't tell me I can't see my friends when I want to," she said. "We had this out a long time ago, remember?"

"Then you will go to Nice and we will see about this Lily afterward."

"You go there to see your family, and I'll visit the Beckers in Nîmes."

The armistice terms designated the south of France the Unoccupied Zone. It was a misnomer—officials of the Vichy regime ruled it—but they in turn were ruled by German overseers.

When Blanche arrived at the Becker farm, a deceptive tranquillity pervaded the countryside. A six P.M. curfew, although it enforced the calm, was one of the few surface signs of the uneasy peace. A tangible sign was the presence of two young enemy soldiers who called regularly on the Beckers and their neighbors to exact a tribute of milk, eggs and vegetables for shipment to Germany. Their demands were always met in silence. Marcel Becker explained that no man, woman or child in the area has said a word to either of the invaders in six months. They accepted the treatment meekly, loaded their truck, and departed with gracious *Auf Wiedersehen*s. But they also kept their revolvers prominently in sight.

171

Marcel smilingly turned down Blanche's offer to help with farm chores. There was very little for him or his wife or daughter to do; they had a small patch of land, a few chickens and a single cow.

"If it weren't for this cursed war," he told her, "we might enjoy the simple life here." There was no anti-Semitic activity in the region, which was "a Godsend."

To while away time and take her mind off the war, Blanche decided to write a film scenario. She meandered across the fields or lounged on the bank of a nearby creek and jotted down her thoughts. A formula mix of characters and scenes filled the notepad.

Her ingenue was "Isabel, a very beautiful but gravely preoccupied young woman of twenty-six." She met "Pierre, a distinguished-looking man of thirty-two, in the waiting room of a Paris fortune-teller."

Isabel and Pierre married after a brief courtship, but because of mistakes made by the young bride, "mistakes that bring ruin to her husband," she ran away.

Thereafter, the plot turned on a series of flashbacks, as Pierre sought his missing bride and unraveled the background that he knew so little about when they were wed. Continuing to be fascinated by a word that she had no reason to apply to herself, Blanche called the story "Jinx" and devoted hours to its development. Inspiration often palled; the story languished, as she did, in a state of inanimation.

"What a fool I was not to see something going on right there," she said later. "I had a real-life story in front of my eyes while I wrestled with myself to manufacture one."

Ariane Becker, teenaged daughter of the household, was wading barefoot into the creek one day when one of the young Germans saw her, kicked off his boots, rolled up his trousers, and splashed in beside her. That evening she told her parents, "He only looked at me, but his eyes were so lonely, so unhappy, I simply had to talk to him. He's just a boy; he's homesick and lost."

They were horror-struck. That night, in the dark, the

young soldier came to the farm with gifts of food that were in short supply. Ariane welcomed him and accepted his offering, but her parents stood rigidly aloof. Then the boy saw a chess set on a table, arrayed for a game. He smiled shyly at Marcel and moved a pawn. The old man had been waiting months to find an opponent. He sat down across from the young enemy soldier, and they began to play.

Although its denouement was still months away, Blanche might have done better than she did with "Jinx" if she had written the story of the French girl and the German boy.

Ignoring a directive to round up all able-bodied Jews and send them to Germany, the boy hid her father and looked after him for more than a year. When the American army drove up from the south, its speedy tanks surrounded the Nazi forces, trapping the two German boys. The villagers fell on one and killed him. But Marcel changed places with the boy who had saved him and hid him in the same place until an American officer offered to protect the young soldier as an honorable prisoner of war.

When Claude came to Nîmes to get Blanche for their return to Paris, she was, in her own words, "nervous as a cat."

"I never want to get off pavement again the rest of my life," she told him. It wasn't just a yearning for Paris streets that gripped her; she was anxious about Lily. Wisely, Claude didn't bring up the subject of forbidding her to see the girl again. He knew it wouldn't do any good.

From her earliest days at the Ritz, Blanche fostered personal relationships with the personnel. The majority responded—maids and busboys, waiters and concierges accepted her foibles, catered to her whims, jumped to attention, and obeyed her wishes. They liked her easy familiarity with their first names; it was André, Edith, Pierre, Monique or whatever, but to them she was always Madame Auzello because they knew that Monsieur le Directeur would want it that way. She made them her devoted friends and, when necessary, accomplices.

On her return from Nîmes, the maids and concierges filled her in on hotel gossip. Topic Number One was that Chanel had returned and was living in her suite again.

Run-of-the-mill man-woman intrigues were taken for granted. They hardly rated the waste of a moment's breath. Woman-woman or man-man live-ins stood higher on a chart of conversational gambits but not much. They were likely to place in the tongue-wagging steeplechase only if such doings were being enjoyed by the celebrated.

In the liberal view of Ritz personnel, it was hardly worth more than passing notice that Coco Chanel was living with two men. What gave added spice, however, was that both her men were known to be actively pro-German.

"She never appeared anywhere in the hotel with either of them," Blanche said. "Nobody gave a damn, but she really worked hard to keep them secret. I knew about them because I had a direct pipeline through the floor maid. She kept me up to the minute. She was envious, not because the Madame was a great couturier—that didn't mean a thing to her; but living with two impressive guys was her idea of paradise. What luxury!"

There were an increasing number of marked men in Paris. The Germans were seeking the leaders of the resistance, and the resistance leaders in turn were tracking down those they considered traitors to their cause. Some had the bad luck to be on both lists. Serge Lifar, one-time star of the Diaghilev Ballet, was one. He hid in Chanel's suite, after being accused of collaboration with the Nazis.

Baron "Spatzy" von Dincklage, who had aroused Claude's ire before the war when he tried to sell wines at black-market prices, was another. Continuing his close relationship with Joachim von Ribbentrop, the dapper German worked actively disseminating anti-French propaganda until he was advised that killer squads of the Maquis looked on him as a choice target for their guns. He prudently avoided them in Chanel's parlor by day and her bed by night.

"I kept running into Coco in the hallway, the lobby, the restaurant," Blanche said. "We exchanged polite talk; she told me about Switzerland, which she said was dull, and I told her about the south of France, which was the same. Naturally, I never let her know that I knew about the men in her apartment, and I didn't dare mention it to Claude, either. I had no idea how he would behave. It would have placed him in a peculiar position, after all. He was so terribly patriotic, he would surely have blown up if he knew 'Spatzy' was being hidden upstairs. But he had that other side to him—regular patrons of the hotel were like members of the deity, and Chanel qualified high up there. He always let his favorites get away with things others could not. I figured that if I knew what was going on, he surely must, too. In other words, I was probably keeping a secret from him that he was keeping from me. Later on, I had reason to believe that Claude always knew everything that went on in the Ritz. And it was lucky for me that he did."

Lily came back into Blanche's life with her usual suddenness. The violets gave an early warning; the small boy simply left the bouquet at the desk and fled. Blanche set out for the bench on the quai, but was only a few yards from the Cambon exit of the hotel when Lily stepped out of a doorway and hugged her gratefully for her swift appearance.

"I had seen many sides of Lily," Blanche said. "I'd seen her mad, happy, sharp, businesslike, full of laughter and glowing with life. This was the first time I ever saw her so distressed."

They walked around the Church of the Madeleine and into an alley off the Boulevard Malesherbes, saying very little to each other because Lily was especially watchful of everyone she saw. Their little spurts of conversation were meaningless; the girl was obviously under too much of a strain to concentrate.

Behind the back door of a tobacco shop, four resistance fighters were crowded in a smelly room not much larger than a clothes closet at the Ritz. Vincenzo was prone on the floor in great pain. He had taken a bullet in his abdomen from a German who was then mowed down. No further details were offered.

Lily said, "I make figure that doctor come get out bullet, then I must move Vincenzo. If he stay here like thees, he die for sure. But not if I give him nursing, which I can do, is right? Of course, you say me yes!"

"What do you mean?"

Lily made her customary gesture of disbelief when confronted by a dense, uncomprehending ally.

"We put in Ritz Hotel. Naturally."

"Would you believe it, I didn't queer that nutty idea? There I was, considering something I knew was impossible. But I was always attracted to the impossible. I remember leading a crusade at school called 'Bring back the dinosaur!' Helping Vincenzo would be like bringing back to life a dinosaur that would trample me to death."

Clearly, they had the utmost faith in her. Lily made them believe her influence in the hotel was so great that all they had to do was deliver Vincenzo and Blanche would do the rest.

"How long would you keep him there?"

Moule, the fellow Blanche had met at the Gare du Nord, shrugged. Another man, a new face to Blanche, said, "A week, a month."

Every impossible task is a dinosaur, she reflected. But this one went beyond impossibility. Lily expected Vincenzo to go through the service entrance to the elevator, then traverse an upstairs corridor and hide in an empty room. Their scheme required that he pass watchmen, floor personnel, and the continually prowling Madame Ritz.

"I might hide him for a night," she conceded. "But a week? Or a month? What about my husband? What happens when he finds out?"

Lily waved that off. "I see how he love you. Fantastic!"

Blanche said, "I can't do it. I'm sorry."

No one stirred for several hour-long moments.

"It's all right," said Lily finally. "We think of other way." She smiled at Blanche, who felt sorry and looked it.

"If there's anything else I can do," she said.

176

"Come tomorrow, yes? We make you another good idea."

She was back the next day at noon. Vincenzo still lay on the floor. The doctor who was to remove the bullet had never shown up.

A swarthy, mustachioed young Spaniard was introduced by Lily with a simple wave of her hand.

"Since Heifer, we don't say no name."

That this new conspirator knew *her* name occurred to Blanche but apparently not to them. The Spanish boy was there to take Vincenzo to the service entrance of the Ritz in a sidecar affixed to his bicycle.

"What about your other plans?" asked Blanche.

There were no others, but they were more anxious than ever to get Vincenzo out of there. German search teams were going through every building in the area. All hotels were being searched, room by room. "But never the Reetz," smiled Lily.

She took it for granted Blanche would agree. "Now I make organized so you no make mistake." She outlined a scheme to get Vincenzo to the hotel's service entrance that evening just before nine o'clock, near the start of the district curfew. It was a propitious hour because the streets filled up with people scurrying for home.

Blanche objected. "That's when the truck delivers its supplies."

"*Completamente,*" said the Spaniard. "You bring here and deliver him to hotel in truck!"

"*Un bon tour, eh? Ca va,* Blanche? Ees great idea!" Lily threw her arms around the boy and kissed him. When the jubilation had died down, they finally saw Blanche shaking her head.

"It won't work," she said. "I'm going to the hotel. If I think of something, I'll be back."

She returned in an hour, hurrying in order to allay their anxieties. They were relaxed, unconcerned, confident she would take care of their problem. They took little notice of her arrival.

The Latin was uncovering components of a short-wave

radio set from a scattering of cigar boxes and cigarette cartons. When he had them together they clustered around to hear.

"Hello, Jeannette; hello, Jean-Pierre. I hope you've been good and obeyed your parents." The announcer went on to broadcast a children's program in which coded instructions were included in songs, innocuous dialogue and the sounds of farm animals. Fifteen minutes later, the afternoon message to the underground finished, the radio was snapped off and dismantled.

There was no message for them, and they were acutely disappointed. "The English, they do nothing all the time," observed Moule in one of the rare times he spoke.

"You no worry," said Lily, with a smile at Blanche. "American mens come soon, you can be sure."

Vincenzo groaned, which brought them back to reality. Reality brought them around to Blanche.

"You've worked in secrecy so long," she said, "you think your every move has to be secret. Well, let's try to get Vincenzo into the hotel as if he belongs there, instead of smuggling him in."

They listened to her, spellbound, nodding their heads in approval.

Just before nine a telephoned message to Claude commanded that he present himself to General von Stulpnagel. "I hated to do it, but we couldn't take a chance that he'd be in the lobby when Lily and Vincenzo came in," said Blanche.

Hobbling on a cane and bravely hiding the pain, Vincenzo arrived on time with Lily. They asked for the key to Room 414 as if they were registered guests already occupying it. The concierge handed it to them. Playing his role like a seasoned actor, he wished Madame and Monsieur a pleasant night's sleep, saw them to the elevator, opened the gate, and manipulated the automatic button that would take them upstairs. When the machine started up, he permitted himself a tiny gesture, a good-luck circle of thumb and forefinger.

Blanche, seated in the lobby, watched them and waited for

Claude to return. "He was roaring mad when he found out it was a phony message. Nobody on the other side knew what he was talking about. But it got him out of the way, and our success depended on that."

Propped up in an enormous bed and with the connivance of friendly personnel, Vincenzo and Lily enjoyed three days of pleasurable living. "Especially I like thees room service," Lily told Blanche. "After the war I go to America and I live like thees. Fantastic."

The doctor appeared, examined Vincenzo and decided that the bullet offered less danger if it remained where it was than if he removed it. The Germans had given up their search of the Madeleine area, and the two young people made ready to depart the next day. Everything had gone smoothly, and the adventure appeared destined to end happily.

"They could have gone out with the doctor," said Blanche. "But they wanted a little more luxury living at the Ritz, and I couldn't blame them."

Next day, the Cambon side of the hotel was alive with German soldiers. An entire squad was deployed outside the entrance and in the lobby. They were to search every room. To Blanche's dismay, she was told they were after a pair of resistance fighters.

She was only slightly relieved to learn that the partisans they sought were not Vincenzo and Lily. Early that morning, two members of a French resistance group had materialized at Chanel's suite and hustled her away. No one knew how they got in, and she, blindfolded, didn't know where she was taken. But three hours later, when her blindfold was removed, she was back upstairs near the door to her suite. She had been questioned about her relationships with Dincklage and Lifar, reminded that collaborators could face disfigurement or death, and told to change her ways. "You are a Frenchwoman," her captors told her, "and an important one. You are good for France, and France has been good to you."

She was undisturbed by the ordeal, but Dincklage was furious. He and General von Stulpnagel wanted Claude to explain how the men got into the hotel, but he maintained that he didn't know any more than they did. Therefore, he couldn't explain it.

The possibility that Chanel's captors were still in the hotel occurred to the Germans, and Claude was ordered to open all doors. Passkeys in hand, he led an officer and six men, their guns drawn, through the corridors.

He also carried the registry list, which he consulted at every door. When he came to their own rooms, Blanche discovered what was going on. She tried to tell him about Vincenzo and Lily in Room 414, but the officer close by his side circumvented her. When they moved on, after inspecting every inch of the Auzello quarters, she sank into a chair, frightened, barely able to breathe.

At Room 414, Claude consulted his list and reported that a honeymoon couple was occupying it. Meanwhile, he was unlocking the door, for the Germans were set to knock it down if he hesitated. He threw it open.

As the men rushed in, Vincenzo rolled away from Lily as if he had been making love to her. But the soldiers riveted their attention on Lily, who sat bolt upright, screaming, naked from the waist up. The officer ordered his men out and, with apologies, gently closed the door.

Later, when the soldiers had left the Cambon side, followed soon afterward by Lily and Vincenzo, Blanche went on the offensive against Claude. "You bastard," she said. "Why didn't you tell me you knew they were there?"

He chuckled. "See here, Blanchette, isn't it time you realize nothing escapes me in the Ritz?"

And still later, Blanche asked Lily what Vincenzo had been doing when he was shot and she saw him on the floor of the tobacco shop.

"He do nothing."

"Then why were they looking for him?"

"They not looking for heem. They look for me!"

She was taking Lily to Maxim's for lunch when those lines were spoken. They were there to celebrate a very special occasion.

The Allied armies had landed in Normandy.

15

Like the Ritz, Maxim's enjoyed the status of an international monument. Occupation and shortages had diminished its gastronomic qualities, but its gaudy fame remained untouched, along with the splendid vulgarity of its Art Nouveau decor.

Taking Lily to lunch there as soon as she knew the allied forces were in France was a true show of defiance, and Blanche knew it. The Germans had seized Maxim's management from owner Octave Vaudable and replaced Maître d' Albert Blaser with a Teutonic replica. They thronged all three dining rooms, but even guttural laughter and a preference for beer over champagne failed to destroy the glorious feeling that Paris could still be Paris.

Reminders of prewar gaiety abounded. Living reminders: the girls who enjoyed the hospitality of their soldier-companions were almost all French. Neither group gave any indication of concern with the Allied invasion, although the BBC let it be known the landings of June 6 were successful and had been secured. It wasn't the end of the war, but a great step toward it, and Blanche decided that day, Saturday, June 10, was a very special day. Any time now, she might see Americans in the Ritz again.

After Lily left the hotel with Vincenzo, the heat of pursuit apparently cooled. She told Blanche, "When this war is over, you will not know who am I. I am changed. I am in the Ritz Hotel always with my diamonds and maybe pearls, too."

"I'll see that a table is reserved for you every day."

"Okay, you make the fun, but you will see. I go always to the

181

Ritz, naturally. But never I have been to the Maxim's. First, I go there."

She persuaded Lily to forgo her more garish display of crazy-quiltish colors that passed for style, tone down her generous use of facial cosmetics, and comb her hair into a semblance of orderliness. Then she spoke aggressive German to the unfamiliar maître d' and procured a table in the most desirable section of the main room.

Lily's immediate interest in the mirrored and red-walled surroundings dissolved away as she surveyed the female "no-goodniks" around her. The laughing, brightly dressed girls and soldiers in spruce green uniforms jam-packed every available space. They visibly depressed Lily.

Three glasses of champagne later, she was her old self. As she gulped the third, she cocked an eye at Blanche and said she was considering an announcement of her presence. What a sensation that would make! Blanche lifted her own third libation in salute.

However, they diverted themselves with a toast to the Allied armies instead, and forgetting her plan for daily postwar attendance at the Ritz, Lily remembered an earlier desire. "After this war, I go to the California and make the film about my *ancien*. You come, too."

She saw that Blanche wasn't following this.

"You big no-goodnik. You have forget Genghis Khan! We are to make the big movie!"

Blanche thought it a most agreeable idea. They emptied their glasses to that future odyssey.

Alongside, smiling cordially, were four German soldiers with two French girls.

"Sit with us," suggested the nearest girl. Their escorts nodded vigorous assent.

Blanche forced a smile and told them in German that they were about to leave. She waved away the waiter she had called to take their order, making a writing motion in the air, the universal signal for her check. Hearing her speak their language made the soldiers even more anxious for their company. Two of them swung their chairs around alongside them, bringing their glasses and a bottle of champagne.

Lily froze. Blanche said later, "I never sobered up so fast in my life." The scene that was about to take place, she was sure, was that they would propose a toast to der Führer and she and Lily would throw the wine in their faces.

It happened almost exactly that way.

But Blanche never raised her glass at all. She let it sit on the table while she stood up and signaled Lily to leave with her.

"*Heil Hitler!*" said the soldier, as he, too, stood up.

Lily, her glass already in her hand, threw its contents into his crotch. Then she and Blanche walked out.

"I couldn't believe they'd let us walk out of there, but they did. I was sure they'd grab us out on the sidewalk, but they didn't. When I got back to the hotel, I really thought I was safe."

Next morning, the Gestapo came and whisked her away.

It wasn't a crisis-type happening that grew easier with repetition, as Claude realized when he learned. There was small comfort in knowing she had so lightly survived her first arrest; each time there would be new dimensions, unknown ramifications, and, for him, excruciating fears.

Like her first time, he had no idea why the Germans had seized her. That made the waiting all the harder. Intensifying his anguish this time, moreover, was the explosive temper of the Germans in Paris. Everyone knew that their Fortress Europa had been breached, the invulnerability of their military might threatened. Overnight, every pleasantry, every smile disappeared.

When they had taken him to jail, he had made a discovery that he had later passed on to Blanche. His jailers sent him to the exercise yard the first morning precisely at eleven o'clock. They marched him past a window that allowed a glimpse of the world outside, and, as a small modicum of joy, he saw her as she sat so disconsolately at the corner café across the street. He didn't see her again, but each morning, like clockwork, they marched him by that window. He could tell by the leaning of shadows that it was always the same time, and besides, such precision was typically German.

After he was released, he told her, "If it happens to me again, you will sit at that café, and when I see you, I will know you are all right."

But now it was she who was inside. Females were allowed to exercise earlier than the male prisoners, so he took up a position at the café at seven each morning and sat there until eleven. He could only hope that she saw him. But she did not; she was miles away, at Fresnes.

She was shackled by an ankle chain to a dozen men and women, and the truck in which they were transported rolled several miles into the suburbs, so she knew it wasn't Santé or Cherche-Midi. A woman next to her identified it; the armed guard riding inside with them allowed the woman to speak. Maliciously, he said, "Say what you like, *fraulein*. While you have breath." Then his shoulders shook with mirth.

Some of her actions at Maxim's came back hazily, and she cursed herself for allowing the wine to get to her. She was determined to face her captors with her usual bravado, but she could not ignore the fact that their mood had changed since her earlier incarceration or that Fresnes was known to be the first stop on the route to the German labor camps. Or worse.

They locked her in a solitary cell, and her first visitor was a benevolent priest. She knew then that her ruse with her passport had worked; they believed her to be Catholic. She thanked him for his solicitude and sent him away, knowing that any interrogation by him would reveal her ignorance of the religion.

When the guard summoned her, he marched her across a prison yard, past rows of prisoners standing motionless, drooping, resembling run-down mechanical toys. She was thrust into a room with other women and made to undress. Her clothes were taken away, and she was given a dirty robe and wooden shoes. Then another guard led her into a prison office where Lily was standing against a wall, her hands and legs encased in metal cuffs.

It flashed into Blanche's mind that members of the resistance were not supposed to recognize each other. But she pulled free, rushed over and embraced her. Then she was yanked away, and before Blanche realized it, Lily had been taken out.

"You are wise to admit knowing her," said the German seated at a desk. There was a clock on the wall behind him and a picture of Adolf Hitler. He dismissed a guard standing by with a rubber truncheon. She watched the action with a deliberate show of contempt. "*Ach so*," she said in a burlesque voice, then went on in German to say that Lily was her friend. "I always know my friends," she told him.

He shrugged and began to read papers on the desk. He looked up and smiled at one point and said, "You are very nonchalant about imprisonment, aren't you?" He was in his early forties, with thinning hair, pale blue eyes set in a cadaverous face. For the first time in four years of war, she was frightened.

He picked up a pen and asked where and when she was born. He noted down Cleveland and the belated date that matched her passport without any reaction.

After a week of incessant questioning, she knew she had reason to be frightened. Accusations against her, all of which she denied vehemently, included charges of harboring enemies of Germany, aiding fugitives, and outright acts of terrorism. With each session she grew more exhausted, so worn out that it wasn't until she was back in her cell that a particularly ominous remark by her interrogator really sank in on her. "I can sentence you to death if I choose, Madame. Presumption of guilt is all I need."

She was momentarily cheered one night when he gave her a package of cigarettes, her brand. They had been brought by Claude. But he wasn't allowed to see her, although she knew other imprisoned wives had been visited by their husbands. She could draw whatever inference she wished from that; the one she drew was not a pleasant one.

Subsequent questionings, although occasionally sarcastic in tone, seemed to her to be rambling and indecisive. She felt reassured by them, believing her captors had nothing on her that could be adjudged serious. But they went on, nevertheless, seemingly with little substance. On and on.

She tried to maintain good behavior, but it wasn't always possible. In frustration she would retaliate and attempt to give her questioner the same treatment he was giving her. She made insulting remarks, as scathing as she could make them, about solitary confinement, filthy food and untreated illnesses in what she called the *abattoir*. He accepted them with composure and even promised to do something about them. But then he did nothing.

He turned away all her questions about Lily, until one morning.

"This friend of yours, Lily—she is Russian?"

"I don't know."

"She is a Russian spy, right?"

"Of course not."

"What does she do? Is she a ballet dancer? A singer? A painter? A writer? She claims to be an artist. What do you say she is?"

"I really don't know."

"But she's your friend. Tell me the truth about her!"

"I am."

"Where did you meet her?"

"On a boat. Coming to France from Egypt. Before the war."

"She came legally? She had a passport?"

"It was at the time of big labor troubles in France. I know I didn't show any papers. There was no one to ask for them."

"You are a very adroit liar, Madame Auzello," he said, and sent her back to her cell.

There were no interrogations for several days, during which Blanche's fears heightened. During that time she heard shooting in volleys in the courtyard, tortured yells through the corridors, and once was shoved past a guard mopping up blood from the floor.

Then . . .

186

"Madame Auzello, I warn you I am losing my patience with you. Now, about this whore who calls herself Lily Kharmay-eff . . ."

"I've told you all I know about her. She is not a whore."

"She is a whore and a Jew."

"No!"

"She is a whore, a Jew, a traitor, a spy, as you well know. I will give you until tomorrow to tell me it's true. If you do, I promise to let you go."

He summoned a guard and said a few indistinct words to him. Then she was marched back to a cell, but it was half the size of the one she had known. There was barely room to stand, and when hours had passed and she was sure it was night, nobody answered her calls or brought food or water.

There was a great deal of action all through the prison that night. She could hear it, even sense it because the floor actually vibrated at times with the weight of man and material in movement.

Sleep was impossible. The unseen activity was unsettling in itself; it turned her thoughts into a scramble of ominous forebodings. She couldn't slow down her brain—it was spinning like an uncontrolled dynamo. It was generating real fever, and by morning she was waging a losing fight against delirium.

"In my lucid moments, I was sure I'd never get out of there alive and would be dead in a day or two. I gave a lot of thought to the life I'd led and the events that had shaped it from year one. I'd had a good life and had few regrets. I was sorry to be leaving Claude.

"Except for that, I was really quite satisfied. I was never a very deep person, I knew that, but I decided that my lack of convictions probably did me more good than harm. I was just a flibbertygibbert, a scatterbrain; I had a hate for Germans—yes, I was strong on that point—but as they were about to kill me I felt they deserved all the hatred I had for them. They hated my family, my mom and pop, my sisters and brothers, just for being Jewish, and I felt that was reason enough to hate them. I had worked myself into a good big hate for them on that account alone when I was pulled to my feet and literally dragged to the interrogation."

It was clear that the prison was almost empty, the corridors free of guards. Shouted orders and marching feet reverberated, coming from the courtyard. Motors were starting and trucks moving out.

She had been held in the prison more than a month, at least that. She knew that much, but not what was transpiring outside. However, that morning, her numbed consciousness recognized the reason for their flight. A strange apparition had loomed up, scary, overpowering. The trauma of defeat. She recognized it because she had seen it before, when it had showed on the faces of the French at Nîmes.

It showed, too, on the face of her questioner, and made his lean features seem uglier than ever to her. She was pushed roughly into a chair, and he began his inquisition, his pen poised over the stack of papers he had written and accumulated in those weeks. That he was proceeding against her at such a moment, under the pressure of chaos and fear around him, amazed her. Apparently spurred by some curious demoniac impulse in his character, he was determined to finish the task he had started.

He pounded away on Lily's Jewishness, sneered at Blanche's shouted denials, and, for the first time, struck her. He bent her arm back to the breaking point and loosened his grasp only when she agreed to tell him the truth.

She was wild-eyed and gasping with pain. He raced back to his side of the desk and started to write. Then he stopped and threw down the pen.

"I am a Jew, not Lily. I was born on the east side in New York, the Jewish section. My name is Rubenstein. My parents came from Germany."

"Madame Auzello! I warn you!"

She said she was using a doctored passport, she had never been in Cleveland in her life. He said he would march her outside and shoot her. They were both on the edge of all rationality when a guard burst in to say the last truck was ready to leave. His words were almost drowned out by Blanche, crying, laughing, insisting she was Jewish.

The guard grabbed her, pushed her toward the door. She screamed and fell back against the wall, sobbing. He looked for instructions from the interrogator.

"We have room. Do we take her?"

The interrogator hesitated, and the guard made a significant move toward his revolver. The interrogator shook his head. He tapped his forehead.

"Mad!" he said. "Let the damned French take care of her. We have better things to do."

She saw and heard it only dimly.

Inexplicably, she was free. She kicked off the wooden shoes and, barefoot, started to walk toward the only place she wanted to be.

The Germans were evacuating men in *Kübelwagens,* motorized carriers fueled by wood-burning furnaces. The pretense of superiority tossed aside, worried rows of troops chugged past, taking no notice of the scarecrow-like woman in black, trudging toward the city.

She used all her strength to try to get to Claude, and it was no use. Finally she stood stock still, unable to move. Then a man came from a house that looked to be unoccupied, spoke to her, and telephoned the Ritz.

Claude had difficulty recognizing her. He assured her it wasn't because she was so changed and had lost so much weight. It was the tears in his eyes—and hers.

She was forty pounds lighter, and nothing in her wardrobe fit. She had to borrow clothes from friends and slender women at work in the hotel. The dimensions of her physical self had been altered by the Nazis, but her spirit remained undaunted.

It was only a matter of days before Paris would be free. Most of the lower-echelon Germans had moved out. Remaining officers and their aides, trying to conclude their own unfinished business, were subject to ambushes. Gunshots were exchanged all over the city between the frightened Germans and the Maquis. Both were trigger-happy.

For Blanche, the certainty that the Allies would arrive was too marvelous to await quietly. She had Claude's permission to go to a corner bistro on the Rue de Rivoli for dinner with the proprietor and his wife.

The food was good, the wine plentiful, and the imminent future so dazzling that it had to be celebrated. When closing time arrived, all were joyously inebriated. The couple offered to walk Blanche back to the Ritz through the blacked-out streets.

Out of that darkness, a German officer approached and asked directions to the Hotel Buckingham. Instantly, Blanche pointed off in the general direction of England and said it was more than four hundred miles away. The German tried to explain he was looking for a hotel of that name and not Buckingham Palace

She pretended she didn't understand, and, having embarked on this pleasant exploit, went on to tell him that Herr Hitler never made it to the British Isles despite his earlier plans. It seemed to her it was a marvelous joke.

"Suddenly I heard footsteps going away," she said. "I looked around, and my friends were running for their lives. I realized then what I was doing: that Nazi could have pulled his gun and killed us all. I was lucky, because he gave a little salute and went off in the dark. I leaned against a wall to keep from fainting."

At dawn, August 24, Paris was awake and making for the parade. Once, in the delectable dream days, the city went to the country for August. But for this one, Blanche and Claude and all the city people didn't want to be anywhere else in the world.

He arranged for them to see it from a room in the Crillon facing the Place de la Concorde, where the triumphant men and machines would wheel in a sort of salute as they marched onto the Rue de Rivoli.

It was usually a ten-minute walk through the connecting streets between the Ritz and the Crillon, but with pushing and shoving and often coming to a full stop when solid humanity blocked the way, it took nearly an hour. There had been shooting and deaths on these very streets in the night. Now they were replaced by cheery noises, voices and laughter, shrill, excited and exuberant, restoring Paris to its precocious enjoyments, the historic position it was meant to occupy on the earth. The early morning that began that final week of August 1944 foreshadowed in Blanche's mind the beginning of a new era of pleasure. There was a great life ahead for her—she intended to make it so; the parade was the curtain going up, the bands were playing the overture, the entertainment had begun.

The parade was magnificent, the flags of different designs, but all with red, white and blue. French veterans proudly showed the way, and then the awesome might of America followed, sprucely uniformed men with tanks and artillery shining as if manufactured yesterday. Blanche gazed down at the first massive gathering of her countrymen she had seen in nearly five years. She leaned dangerously out the open window, screaming *"Le Boche est fini!"* over the roar of the tanks so loudly that Claude had to urge calm, but again and again the same shout burst from her.

At the end of the line of march, the Hôtel de Ville, the infantry disbanded and spilled into the populace. Claude and Blanche left the Crillon, he to hurry back to his duties at the Ritz while she started for the Avenue Montaigne and her apartment. She had instructed Elise to pull out all her liquor from its hiding place. She was going to gather up some GI's and throw a party.

She started walking down the Champs-Elysées, keeping to the shade of the trees, stopping at times to sit and enjoy the enormous movement that swirled around her. Numerous GI's went by, hustling back to the Etoile and the delectable females they had seen there. God, she thought, how young they look. They never even looked at her, the hollow-eyed middle-aged lady in the coarse black cotton dress and stockings. How would they know that all the cares of the war years had fallen away from her that morning? That in this solitude in a crowd she was reflecting on silks and perfumes and champagne? She rose up suddenly, as if the old life could no longer wait to be reborn.

Five GI's approached. Their leader's French had a provincial accent. "South Boston," she decided.

"Pardonnez-moi," he was saying. *"Voulez-vous une bière?"* Beer was the key word; all pounced on it and pronounced it badly. It was a very hot day, and they were in acute need. They opened their mouths and pointed to their tonsils and clamored, *"Bière! Bière!"*

Her smile baffled them, but it was just too good an occasion to cut short.

"I stood there with my hands on my hips and let them suffer a moment, then out of sheer joy I laughed in their faces and said, 'Why don't you bastards speak English?' "

Aftermath

"When you outlive a war, you know what really counts."
—Blanche Auzello

Perhaps the Germans hoped against hope, perhaps they hated to leave Paris, but they waited until the last possible moment—until the liberators were at the gates—before they quit the hotel.

Then, their dignity gone with their pride, they carried out linen, silverware, even upholstered chairs to their waiting vehicles.

Alerted, Claude deployed employees in adjacent doorways, and as the looters hurried back for more, his men ran out and retrieved what had already been taken. The Germans raced away with only what they could grab on their last sweep of the rooms.

At last, Claude could move at will through corridors denied him for five years.

Eager to restore the elegance and luxury that were the war's earliest casualties, he inspected every room from the floor up to audit future needs.

He found a fully loaded handgun in a closet and put it in a drawer in his desk.

"If your enemy takes something, it's loot," he told associates, chuckling. "If you do, it's a souvenir."

As soon as the American embassy reopened, Blanche took her passport, so painstakingly altered, for renewal. She was incensed when the woman in charge stared at the lapsed date, stamped it VOID, and wouldn't give it back. She phoned Congressman Sol Bloom in Washington and told him, "This nutty lady must think the Nazis should have renewed it for me." In a

193

few days the embassy sent word that a valid passport was waiting.

She said, "I want that same woman to hand it to me." More calls to Washington and it was done. "A little ceremony I dreamed up for myself," she said.

Indulgently, Claude escorted Blanche back to her table in the bar, to her cherished place facing the door, where she could watch for friends.

Fashion designer "Foxy" Sondheim (the mother of composer-lyricist Stephen Sondheim) was in a contingent flown over by the State Department soon after V-E Day.

"I had read Walter Winchell's story that Blanche was killed by the Nazis," she said. "I went to the Ritz and was asking if Claude was in the hotel when I heard my name called. It was Blanche, and when I saw her I nearly fainted. She was like a skeleton, but otherwise she was her old self."

Blanche wasted no time shaking off the hardships of war, and Claude observed this with a blend of love and amusement. "Look here, she had been cast away on a desert island for five years. Food, clothing and shelter were our basic needs; we had no use for jewelry, fine fashions and big limousines. Blanche missed them, of course. She felt she had been robbed and wanted them back."

He was happy to see her anticipation that the past could be restored. She was in the bar every afternoon, wearing the finest the fashion houses could provide, her hair newly coiffed, legs in comfortable nylon, strings of pearls around her neck.

"It was her nature to believe she would soon get back everything the war years took away. It was not mine to be so optimistic," concluded Claude.

Prince J'Ali was among those who reappeared. He was in a hospital and begged Blanche to come see him. "You must, my angel." Accompanied by a friend, Selma Jenny, Blanche went hesitantly to call on her former lover.

"If he wasn't in the hospital, I wouldn't have gone," she said. A fashionably trimmed beard added to his appeal. In scarlet

194

silk Turkish pajamas, he displayed all his remembered charm and honeyed words at the sight of her.

Their talk turned back the clock, ticking off the good old days in New York. And nights. He recalled how good he was in bed. There had been good nights in Paris, too. J'Ali reached inside his pajama top and brought out the talispiece that contained her lock of hair.

"It is as I told you, my angel. It is always close to the beating of my heart."

In the midst of their remembrances, a pretty girl came into the room, a flashy creature in a red and blue wool outfit. Her skirt was short, and she had long, silky legs. She could have been Blanche a quarter-century before.

She bestowed an affectionate kiss on the man in the bed, while Blanche wondered if she was his daughter. Or even his granddaughter.

"This is Jeanne," he told his visitors. "My beautiful fiancée."

As they were leaving the hospital, Blanche said to Selma, with a smile, "What will you bet that buzzard stuck the locket in his shirt when he knew I was coming?"

As usual, Claude asked if she enjoyed the day. There was a temptation to tell him. Then she could explain it right through to the end. But she decided against it, simply saying she and Selma did some shopping.

There was no point in letting Claude believe she felt any emotion at all about the Prince. She would never mention him again. The curtain was down.

For months, Marie Louise Ritz appeared only occasionally in the dining room, and then she was on the arm of a nurse. She enjoyed a glass of Lafite, a bottle from her private stock always on her table. When she finished her meals, she had the maître d' carefully mark the level of wine left in the bottle. The last time she was to dine there it was almost empty. She passed away as quietly as she lived.

When the war criminal trials at Nuremberg ended with ten executions and two suicides, Claude said, with pretended sadness, "We have lost twelve steady customers."

But there were other faces he sincerely missed, and pleasant voices that would never be heard again.

It was Blanche who clung desperately to the hope that her life at the Ritz could be the same again.

She kept watch for many, among them Lily Kharmayeff. But after their embrace in the prison at Fresnes, she never saw her again.

Some of the rich and social figures, statesmen and leftovers of royalty trickled into the hotel after the shooting stopped. By the early 1960s the stream was running faster.

Flags of many nations flew over the entrance to proclaim the presence of the celebrated from all the continents.

Suddenly, expected American guests failed to arrive. Their cancellations fluttered down on Claude's desk from London, Brussels, Madrid, Rome and, to add insult to frustration, the resorts of Germany.

The emotional love affair between France and the United States was over. France's new president Charles de Gaulle was spreading a campaign of hate against Americans, and his shadow all but blotted out the façade of the Ritz.

After he officially recognized Red China, the Stars and Stripes was put away in the porter's closet for long periods.

Inspired with a latent affection for the hotel, slim, forceful and impeccably stylish Charley Ritz, his seventieth birthday behind him, came briskly through the portals. He was in fine physical shape and excellent humor. As heir to his mother's estate, he had netted the biggest catch of his life, executive mastery of the hotel.

He was still enamored of the modern improvements he had seen in the great hotels of the United States and brushed aside Claude's argument that de Gaulle was keeping Americans away.

"It is because they are accustomed to conveniences that are not here," he said. "You've allowed the hotel to fall behind the times."

He still had no use for the traditions of César Ritz and spoke of installing dial phones, radios and even television in the rooms. He contemplated high-speed elevators. Claude argued fruitlessly.

Charley decided he would first change the decor of the Cambon side of the hotel. The Grill Room was refurbished, and Charley, ever the fisherman, renamed it L'Espadon, the swordfish. Then he brought in workmen and changed the looks and lighting of the bar. Blanche felt homeless during the weeks it was closed. Bartender Georges Scheuer quit.

"I wish I had your independence," Claude told him. "But you do not have Blanche."

To Blanche he said, "Charley is a tough one. I no longer have the strength to fight him. I am very sad." However, he summoned up a flash of humor and told her, "If he tries to put frozen foods in our kitchens, I will punch his jaw."

He tried to make her understand that times had changed and the era of elegance was over. "Maybe so," she said. "Perhaps the good old days *are* gone, but I'm not!"

He tried to keep from her how Charley was taking away his authority, how he had diverted the incoming mail in order to handle the reservations that meant so much to him. When she noted his rising despondency, he suggested he might retire and they could live in the Villa Linda in Nice. But she wasn't interested.

"Look here," he told her, "we have had what we wanted out of life. Let us be satisfied."

"No," she said. "I won't let Charley move us out of the hotel. He wouldn't have a hotel if it weren't for you."

The relationship between the two men deteriorated. Its reverberations spread, and there were outpourings of sympathy from Claude's associates, who saw that he was caught between his boss, who wanted him out, and his wife, who wanted him to stay.

His talk of retirement was only halfhearted. His own fierce love for the hotel added to his uncertainties, and he was not sure he *could* leave.

He was aging noticeably, but Blanche, too, was showing her years, and that compounded his unhappiness. He conveyed his feelings in phone calls to relatives in the south, nephews and a niece, long distant, suddenly close when there was no one else in Paris to turn to.

His conversations included curious comments, disjointed, tinged with the laments of a man losing control of everything dear to him. His reverence for both loves was tearing him apart.

"Charley is treating me like I am a bellhop. . . .

"Blanche is most difficult. She no longer listens to reason. . . .

"I am in the depths of melancholia. . . ."

Nobody interpreted it as a cry for help. They knew what a fighter he was, even when the battle went badly.

One day, Blanche suffered a fainting spell as she was leaving the hotel and was carried back into the lobby. When she came to, after fifteen minutes of unconsciousness, she couldn't remember anything about it. She was disinclined to have treatment, especially when a conclave of doctors was unable to diagnose the cause. One of the physicians, hardly more than a boy, recommended that she quit drinking.

She said, "He's young. He wouldn't know." She went off to a beauty parlor, and more fainting spells followed.

Claude was panicked. He pleaded with her not to go out alone. Her loyal housekeeper, Elise, traveled to Lourdes to pray for her, and it seemed to all of them that God was listening. Blanche's health showed improvement.

In the late 1960s, when de Gaulle and France were involved with rebellious Algeria, the attitude of the French toward the United States softened. Americans ventured back, but their own problems in Southeast Asia left them uneasy. Talk of a third world war kept the hotel's guests in uneasy postures, like long distance runners on the mark, waiting for the starting gun.

Claude felt certain that this state of affairs would convince Blanche she could never recapture the elegant past. "It is related to the malaise of the times," he said.

His contract as Managing Directeur was still in force, but his days were empty and he had no voice in the hotel's operation.

198

He spoke of retirement with greater feeling, but she still opposed it.

"Look here," he growled, "I tell you it is impossible to hold what we have had and too late to look for more. You're the most difficult woman I have ever known!"

"You knew that when you asked me to marry you," she told him sweetly. When moments like that passed, dissension between them also melted away; he didn't want her to bear any more misery than necessary.

She could look back wistfully to the days when she had been amused by the women who tried so desperately to retain their youth. Now it was she who held to that hopeless fantasy.

She had put on weight; a postwar craving led her to joke that she enjoyed a cup of sugar with two lumps of coffee.

She selected a deep brunette color for her hair. "It matches the dark corners of my soul," she said.

It took hours after she awoke each day before she lost the hoarseness in her voice. After one phone conversation with a shopkeeper, she jammed the receiver and said, "God damn it, every time I talk on the phone in the morning they call me 'Monsieur.' "

She agreed to allow a Russian artist to paint a full-length portrait of her, then tried to erase the lines in her face with a crayon. When that failed, she grabbed an ice pick. The painter fled. But she didn't mean to use it on him—she stabbed it through the canvas.

In a call to Jean Graniou, a beloved nephew and successful industrialist in Nice, Claude started with "I am very sad." Graniou offered to come to Paris, bring his two sons, and have a whirl with him through some remembered places. But Claude told him, "No. Stay with your children. Be happy with them. They will bring you true happiness."

In April, saying it was time to rearrange their lives, he dismissed Elise and engaged a *femme de chambre* from the Ritz to replace her on a part-time basis. He and Blanche would be alone in the apartment at night.

Only with the gift of hindsight would anyone see that the words and actions revealed suicidal melancholia. But then, clues that lead to tragedy commonly come to light afterward. Among the items he transferred to the apartment from the hotel was the German handgun he had kept in his office since the liberation of Paris.

On the last day of her life, Blanche said, "At last, Claude and I have a marvelous relationship. We are closer than either of us ever thought we could be. We regret every hour we've spent apart."

About three in the morning, May 29, 1969, a neighbor was awakened by a loud report. He thought it was a tire blowout. Three hours later he heard another.

The new maid fixed breakfast, then waited. Finally she peeped into the bedroom. Blanche looked to be asleep. The girl started to close the door. Then she saw Claude on the floor, clutching the gun in his inert hand, and she ran out screaming.

Index